GENUINE JAPANESE ORIGAMI

34 Mathematical Models Based Upon √2

BOOK 2

Jun Maekawa

Translated by Koshiro Hatori

DOVER PUBLICATIONS, INC.
Mineola, New York

Bibliographical Note

This Dover edition, first published in 2012, is a new English translation and a new selection of models from *Genuine Origami √2*, originally published by Japan Publications, Inc., Japan, in 2009.

Genuine Japanese Origami, Book 1 is available as a Dover edition (0-486-48331-2).

International Standard Book Number
ISBN-13: 978-0-486-48335-1
ISBN-10: 0-486-48335-5

Manufactured in the United States by Courier Corporation
48335501
www.doverpublications.com

Fold everyday sheets and use in everyday life.

Plate (page 32)

Octagon Wrapper (page 34)

Money Gift Wrapper (page 20)

Yin Yang Box (page 21)

Trash Bin (page 27)

Box with Cat Ears (page 105)

Diagonally-Opening Gift Cube (page 107)

Box with Handles (page 109)

Cube Masu Box (page 111)

*Non-sunken Honeycomb
Octahedron (page 46)*

√2 is the carpenters' number.

House (page 86)

L-shaped House (page 88)

Re-roofing (page 90)

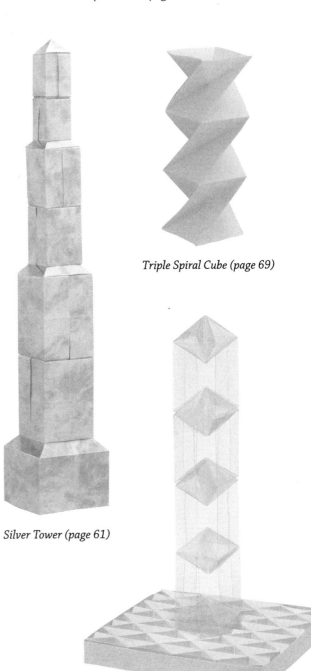

Triple Spiral Cube (page 69)

Silver Tower (page 61)

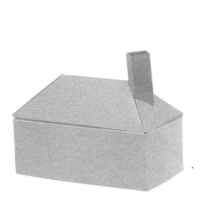

Hip Roof (page 98)

Silver Honeycomb (page 65)

The key for the puzzle is √2.

*Honeycomb
Octahedron (page 40)*

*One-sheet Honeycomb
Octahedron (page 43)*

*Honeycomb Octahedron in
Coordinate System (page 48)*

*Honeycomb Octahedron in
Intersecting Square Prisms (page 50)*

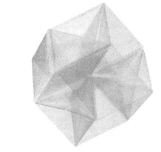

Inverted Cube: Rhombic Dodecahedron and Cube Skeleton (page 53)

*Two-sheet Sunken Rhombic
Dodecahedron (page 57)*

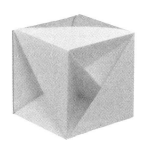

Loop Hole Cube (page 71)   *Half Z Cube (page 73)*   *Plug-and-socket Puzzle Cube (page 76)*   *One-third Cube (page 79)*

Penta-hepta-hexahedron (page 102)   *Iso-area Half-cooked Cube (page 118)*   *Hexa-roofed Polyhedron (page 83)*

Cube Rose (page 114)   *The Die Is Split (page 123)*   *Iso-area Hexa-cube (page 120)*

PREFACE

Despite being a continuation of *Genuine Origami* published in 2008, this book is titled *Genuine Japanese Origami: 34 Mathematical Models Based Upon √2* rather than *Genuine Origami 2* because it includes origami models that are made of rectangle sheets with aspect ratio around 1:1.41 or 1:√2, the most common sheets used internationally in everyday life.

It is not generally known that origami conceals one of its richest veins in the rectangle with this aspect ratio. We have some traditional models made of rectangular sheets with proportions close to the ratio. In the modern era, some pioneers such as Eiji Nakamura and Koya Ohashi have explored this field of origami, and Kunihiko Kasahara recently published a series of enjoyable books titled *Chohokei-de Oru (Folding Rectangles)*.

I myself have also designed many origami models using these proportions. Whereas many regard the square as canonical in origami, I find "harmony of form," which is the most important appeal of origami for me, in many figures other than the square. Among them, I am fascinated by the 1:√2 rectangle no less than the square.

Moreover, the number √2 itself is so fascinating that some have written books dedicated exclusively to it. I have also included in this book some mathematical topics about the number. Since I am not an expert in math or math education, I have limited them to those that are interesting to me and have something to do with the origami models, so that I will not annoy you. As a fan of mathematics, however, I would be pleased if you enjoy amusing mathematics, different from painful mathematics taught at school, by reading them along with folding paper.

So, welcome to the beautiful world of √2.

Even when we play, we must do it seriously to enjoy it.
—Teiji Takagi, from *Sugaku Shokei (Small Landscape of Mathematics)*

A white square
In a
White square
In a
White square
In a
White square
In a
White square
In a
White square

Excerpt from Katsue Kitazono's poem *Tancho-na Kukan (Monotonous Space)* in *Kemuri-no Chokusen (Lines of Smoke)*

CONTENTS

INTRODUCTION

The book contains origami models that are made from the 1:√2 rectangle with some exceptions, and consists of these three chapters:

Chapter 1: Paper Shapes and √2
Chapter 2: √2 and 22.5°
Chapter 3: Genuine Origami[3]—√2 and the Cube

Chapter 1 is rather a long introduction that describes the 1:√2 rectangle, which is the theme of the book, taking some models as examples. I recommend at least looking through "Paper Selection" on the next page and "Paper Sizes" at the beginning of Chapter 1 to understand the aspect ratio of paper before you start folding.

In Chapter 1, I will explain four properties of the 1:√2 rectangle: it has matching angles; it is the most common rectangle; it relates to the cube; and it has repeating structures.

Relatively easy "angle-matching" models will be diagramed in Chapter 2.

Chapter 3 has an array of puzzle-like models pertaining to the cube. That is the reason why the title of the chapter is raised to the power of 3.

I have inserted some tips for making models and columns regarding them, presented in boxes like this one, into the diagrams. Some of the columns relate to background information about the models rather than making them.

You can, of course, skip reading the columns and start to make any models you like without paying attention to the order of the book.

I have omitted detailed explanations of folds and techniques. I am sure, however, that you will be able to enjoy the book by itself. When you stumble upon a step, look up the symbols and basic folds, and observe the diagram of the next step. Reading the instructions will also help you solve the problem.

PAPER SELECTION

To make models in the book, you will need to use sheets in international standard sizes, whose ratio of the longer side to the shorter one is around $\sqrt{2}$ (about 1.414), rather than square origami paper. You can use copy paper, letter paper, flyer, notepad, or other kinds of paper of this aspect ratio.

Refer to the beginning of Chapter 1 (page 14) for details about the standard paper sizes.

Although you can use generic A4 copy paper for most models in this book, I have specified the best paper size for each model, such as A4 or A5. You can obtain two A5 sheets by cutting one A4 sheet in half, as the numbers in the names of standard sizes rise by 1 every time they become half their size.

You may be able to purchase different types of standard-sized paper at large stores. At the end of this book, I have appended information about the paper I used for the models in the pictures at the beginning of the book.

One type of paper I recommend is 50–70 g/m^2 craft paper as it is relatively easy to obtain and good to fold. It is used for brown envelopes and other purposes.

You can also use sales flyers or wrapping paper, though you need to check the aspect ratio because such sheets do not tend to come in standard sizes. I have explained how to check the aspect ratio at the beginning of Chapter 1 (page 14).

This box is in the same size as an A6 sheet (105 x 148 mm).

This box is in the same size as a JIS B6 sheet (128 x 182 mm).

This box is in the same size as an A5 sheet (148 x 210 mm).

SYMBOLS AND BASIC FOLDS

I have adopted the standard set of symbols used in many origami books.

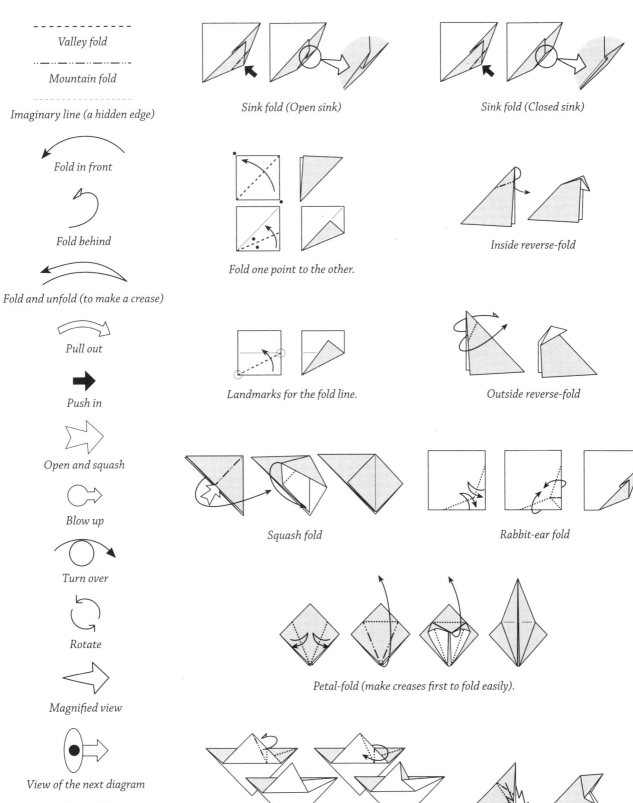

Valley fold

Mountain fold

Imaginary line (a hidden edge)

Fold in front

Fold behind

Fold and unfold (to make a crease)

Pull out

Push in

Open and squash

Blow up

Turn over

Rotate

Magnified view

View of the next diagram

Repeat the steps (at step numbers)

Sink fold (Open sink)

Sink fold (Closed sink)

Fold one point to the other.

Inside reverse-fold

Landmarks for the fold line.

Outside reverse-fold

Squash fold

Rabbit-ear fold

Petal-fold (make creases first to fold easily).

Two types of swivel folds.

(Outside) Crimp

1 PAPER SHAPES AND √2

The square looks too symmetric to be stable, doesn't it?

—Tsuyoshi Mori in *Sugaku Daimyojin (God of Mathematics)*
by Tsuyoshi Mori and Mitsumasa Anno

1. PAPER SIZES

ASPECT RATIO OF STANDARD SIZES

In Japan, paper sizes are standardized as shown in the table on the right, so that the ratio of the longer side to the shorter one is almost √2 (about 1.414). Then, one half of a sheet is always geometrically similar (having the same proportions) to the original shape because of this formula.

$$\frac{\sqrt{2}}{2} = \frac{1}{\sqrt{2}}$$

The size of A0 is defined so that the area is 1 m², and the area of JIS B0 is 1.5 m². The other sizes are determined by cutting them in half.

CHECKING THE ASPECT RATIO

Although most of the sheets around us are in standard sizes, there are many non-standard sheets of paper and sheets in different standards. In making models in the book, you need to use sheets with accurate proportions. You can check the aspect ratio by folding your sheet in the way shown below. This method works because a square has a diagonal of length √2.

	A Series	B Series
0 (full size)	841 x 1189	1030 x 1456
1	594 x 841	728 x 1030
2	420 x 594	515 x 728
3	297 x 420	364 x 515
4	210 x 297	257 x 364
5	148 x 210	182 x 257
6	105 x 148	128 x 182
7	74 x 105	91 x 128
8	52 x 74	64 x 91
9	37 x 52	45 x 64
10	26 x 37	32 x 45

JIS Standard Paper Sizes (mm x mm)

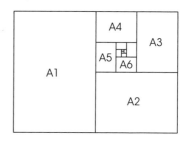

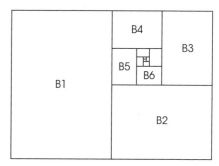

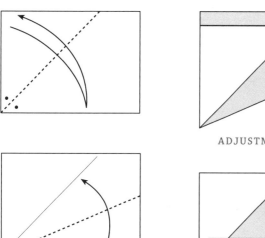

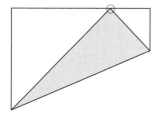

The aspect ratio is "correct" if the corner precisely sits on the edge.

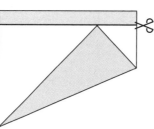

ADJUSTMENT: CASE 1

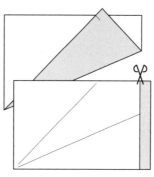

ADJUSTMENT: CASE 2

CUTTING OUT A 1:√2 RECTANGLE FROM A SQUARE

Many of you probably already have origami paper. You can cut out a 1:√2 rectangle sheet from a square sheet by following figures 1–4.

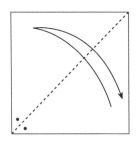

PAPER CUTTER

A letter opener will work very well to cut out smaller sheets such as A5. Some models in the book even require cutting paper into strips.

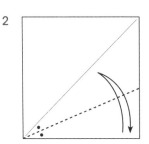

SILVER RECTANGLE

The 1:√2 rectangle is sometimes called "silver rectangle," contrasting with the golden ratio that is about 1:1.618. The silver ratio, however, generally refers to 1:1+√2 rather than 1:√2.

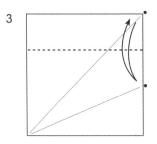

LETTER SIZE

Although it is an international standard, the √2-based A series is not common in North America. Rather, letter size paper A4 Letter Size 11 inch = 279.4 mm is widely used, whose size is close to A4. Its aspect ratio is 8.5:11 or about 1.294.... 8.5 inch = 215.9 mm

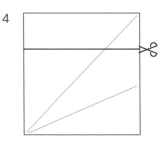

B SERIES

The JIS (Japanese Industrial Standards) B series, defined so that the area of B0 is 1.5 m^2, is a Japanese original standard. It is based on another Japanese standard Mino-ban (9 sun x 1 shaku 3 sun), the official standard size in the Edo period (1603–1868). The standard size of books made of Mino-ban sheets is called Shiroku-ban (4 sun 2 bu x 6 sun 2 bu), and it is close to JIS B5. (Shaku, sun, and bu are old Japanese units of length. 1 shaku is almost the same length as 1 foot, 1 sun is a tenth of 1 shaku, and 1 bu is a tenth of 1 sun.)

On the other hand, ISO (International Organization for Standardization) has defined its B series so that B0 is 1000 x 1414 mm, which is slightly smaller than JIS B0. The less-known ISO C series is defined as the geometric mean (the square root of the product) of A and B series. Therefore, the size of C0 is 917 x 1297 mm ($917 \approx \sqrt{841 \times 1000}$).

A4   *Letter size*

8.5 inch = 215.9 mm

11 inch = 279.4 mm

OTHER STANDARDS IN JAPAN

Another Japanese paper size whose proportions are different from 1:√2 is Hanshi, literally translated into "half paper," so called because it is originally the half size of large Sugihara-gami. It generally refers to the size around 7 x 9 sun, and its aspect ratio is 1.2–1.3.

Sheets for Japanese newspapers are also not in the silver rectangle. The standard size is 546 x 406.5 mm and called "blanket-ban," named after the standard size of the rotary press. Its aspect ratio is about 1.343.

Most of the standard sizes for books in Japan, e.g. Kiku-ban and Shiroku-ban, are close to, but usually somewhat different from, the silver rectangle. So, make sure to use silver rectangle sheets in making models in the book.

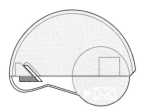

My favorite letter opener:
Midori Letter Cutter

2. SILVER RATIO

HISTORY OF THE PAPER-SIZE STANDARD IN JAPAN

The current Japanese paper-size standard was established in 1929 after the German standard at that time, which is said to have been proposed by the Nobel Prize in Chemistry winner Friedrich W. Ostwald (1853–1932).

Before the standardization, there were some de facto standards in Japan. I have counted the aspect ratio of paper enrolled in *Shokoku Shimeiroku (Catalogue of Paper from All Over Japan)* published in 1877 to make the bar chart on the right. You can see a peak near the silver ratio, though the chart is not technically relevant because I have not taken the production volume into account. Another peak at 1.25 corresponds to the Hanshi described on the previous page. In addition, the paper in the collection of Shosoin, Nara, which was probably made in the eighth century, also has the aspect ratio of around 1.4. On the other hand, the aspect ratio of Chinese paper from 100 BCE is about 1.6.

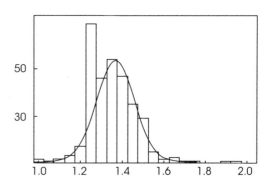

A count of the aspect ratio of Japanese paper enrolled in Shokoku Shimeiroku *(1877)*

Also interesting is an essay written by Ota Nampo (1749–1823) c. 1800.

> When the width of a book is six sun measured with a steel square, the height should be six sun with the back side of the square. The width and height should be in the same measurement with the front and back sides of a square. The height of the title piec e should be two thirds of the book, and the width one sixth. Not only books but also boxes and other rectangle things will look good in the same measurement with the front and back sides.
>
> *Hannichi-kanwa (Half-day Idle Talk)*

A steel square is not merely a measuring tool but also a kind of calculator. The back side of a Japanese steel square has scales that are either 3.14 times (round scales) or 1.414 times (square scales) longer than those on the front side. Nampo referred to a steel square with square scales, which means he asserted that the aspect ratio of a book should be 1:√2. That is one of the oldest propositions on the aspect ratio, if not on the paper size. Another proposition can be found, interestingly, on the opposite side of the world. The contemporary German physicist Georg C. Lichtenberg insisted on the same thing referring to the paper size in his letter in 1786.

SILVER AND GOLDEN RATIO

The reason why Nampo advocated the silver ratio was not that using it was rational because its half is similar to the original shape, but that it looked good for him. In fact, some say Japanese generally prefer the silver ratio (about 1:1.414) to the golden ratio (about 1:1.618, also see the column on page 68). I refer to 1:√2 as the silver ratio, whereas, as I have mentioned, some refer to 1:1+√2.

The graphic science expert Koji Miyazaki, for example, presumes that the facial proportions of Japanese and Western beauties agree with the silver and golden ratio, respectively. It is also known that the buildings and corridors of the Horyuji in Japan have been built according to the silver ratio, whereas the Parthenon in Greece has been designed according to the golden ratio. Taking the Japanese steel square into consideration, I am sure that, in a sense, traditional Japanese architects believed in the silver ratio. Though Chinese have also been using similar steel squares since ancient times, Japanese sometimes revere Prince Shotoku holding a steel square as a god of carpenters.

The silver ratio is sometimes called "Japanese ratio" or "Japanese golden ratio," for which we have good reasons.

The mathematician Shigeru Nakamura has presented interesting statistics on the preferred proportions of rectangles in his book *Fibonacci-su-no Sho-uchu (Fibonacci Numbers' Microcosm)*, from which I have made the charts on the right. You can see a steep peak at the golden ratio in the chart for Germans of 150 years ago. On the other hand, Japanese today prefer the silver ratio best of all. Also notable is that many Japanese prefer the square, although as many do not. Such bias would be much stronger among origami enthusiasts.

I could go on with many more topics about the silver ratio.

For example, Susumu Sakurai, an active writer in math education and other fields, has suggested that the seven and five syllables of Haiku may relate to the silver ratio. In fact, the ratio 7:5 is close to it. Japanese use seven and five syllables in many phrases besides Haiku, even in a mnemonic rhyme for remembering the decimal representation of $\sqrt{2}$.

I would, however, agree with the mathematician Tsuyoshi Mori's opinion that the forms of Japanese verse are derived from powers of 2, that is, 4, 8 and 16. Nonetheless, I have included one origami model that utilizes the ratio 7:5, *Penta-hepta-hexahedron*, in the book. Actually, I was very pleased when I discovered it.

ORIGAMI USING SILVER RECTANGLES

What I want to say with the rather long list of trivia is that the silver rectangle is "beautiful," and that the theme of the book is taking "beautiful" forms out of it. As I have said in the preface, there are some traditional models made from the silver rectangle, and we have some pioneers of the silver rectangle origami, such as Eiji Nakamura, Koya Ohashi, and Kunihiko Kasahara. Nakamura even calls the silver rectangle "the true rectangle."

> The true rectangle no doubt conceals many more secrets. I hope you will discover new laws and properties of it by watching and folding true rectangle sheets.
>
> (Eiji Nakamura, *Soratobu Origami Kessaku 30-sen*
> (*30 Selections of Origami Masterpieces That Fly*), 1973)

This book is, in a sense, my answer to his call.

In addition, Kasahara has recently presented a lot of brilliant models using silver and longer rectangles in his recent book series *Fold with Rectangles* and thus proven the high potential of silver rectangle sheets as origami paper.

On the basis of such results, I would like to add my own models designed from my standpoint as a fan of geometry puzzles. Indeed, the silver rectangle really matches with puzzles.

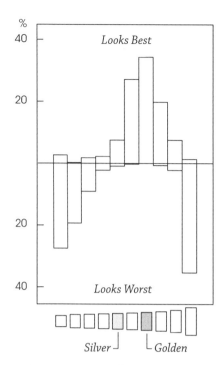

Survey On Preferred Rectangles Conducted by Gustav Fechner in the 1860s.

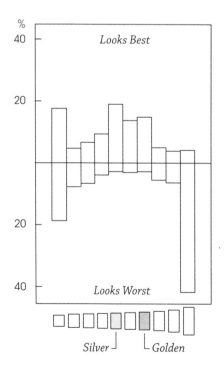

Survey of 250 Japanese on Preferred Rectangles Conducted by Shigeru Nakamura in 2001.

3. SQUID AIRPLANE (TRADITIONAL) AND MONEY GIFT WRAPPER

TRADITIONAL MODELS

First, let's look at the rectangle origami in general taking a traditional model as an example. Traditional models are anonymous origami models that have been passed down hand by hand. Among them, *Squid Airplane, Navel Airplane, Boat, Hat, Banger, Box,* and others are made of rectangle sheets.

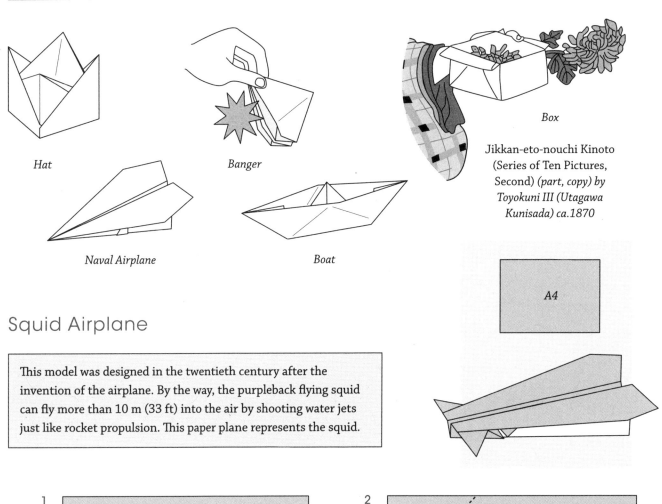

Hat

Banger

Box

Naval Airplane

Boat

Jikkan-eto-nouchi Kinoto
(Series of Ten Pictures,
Second) *(part, copy) by
Toyokuni III (Utagawa
Kunisada) ca.1870*

A4

Squid Airplane

This model was designed in the twentieth century after the invention of the airplane. By the way, the purpleback flying squid can fly more than 10 m (33 ft) into the air by shooting water jets just like rocket propulsion. This paper plane represents the squid.

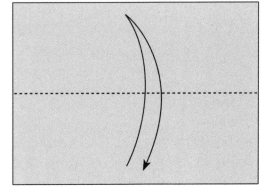

1

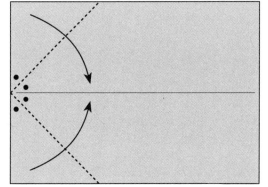

2

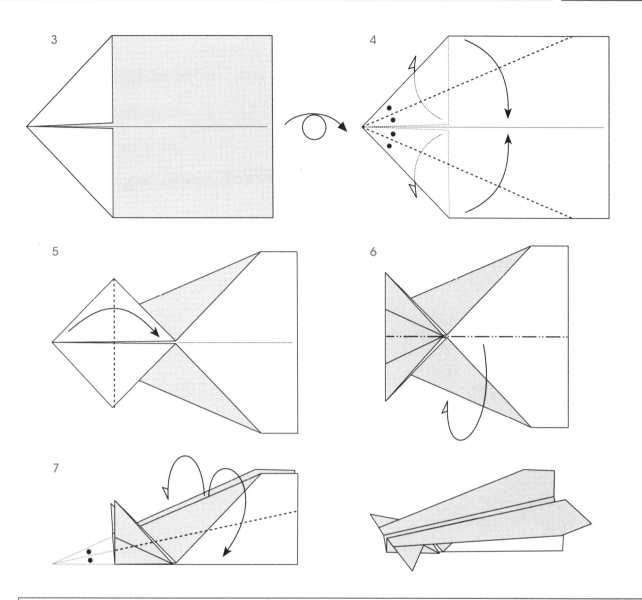

ASPECT RATIO FOR THE SQUID AIRPLANE

I find it clumsy that the diagonal creases in the *Squid Airplane* do not hit the corners indicated in the figure on the right. Don't you feel the plane has "extra length?" If you want to make the creases hit the corners, you should use a rectangle sheet with proportions about 1:1.207 as shown in the middle figure on the right. I made one for some test flights and found that it flies very well with some adjustment for the angle of its wings. That means we do not have to use a silver rectangle sheet for the *Squid Airplane*. We can use any rectangle sheets whose aspect ratio is around 1:1.4. It is also the case for the traditional models named on the previous page.

JOY OF FINDING SHAPES

Examining the extra length further, you may find that it is not just extra. When you fold this part edge-to-edge as shown in the bottom figure on the right, the apices of the two triangles will meet each other at the point indicated by the white circle. Moreover, you will have a white square that is in the same size as the one on the left. These shapes inspired me to design *Money Gift Wrapper* shown on the next page. One of the joys of origami is to discover the harmony of forms.

Extra Length?

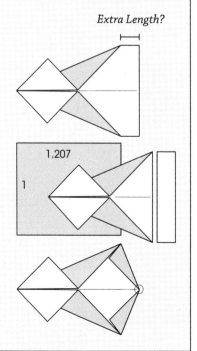

Money Gift Wrapper

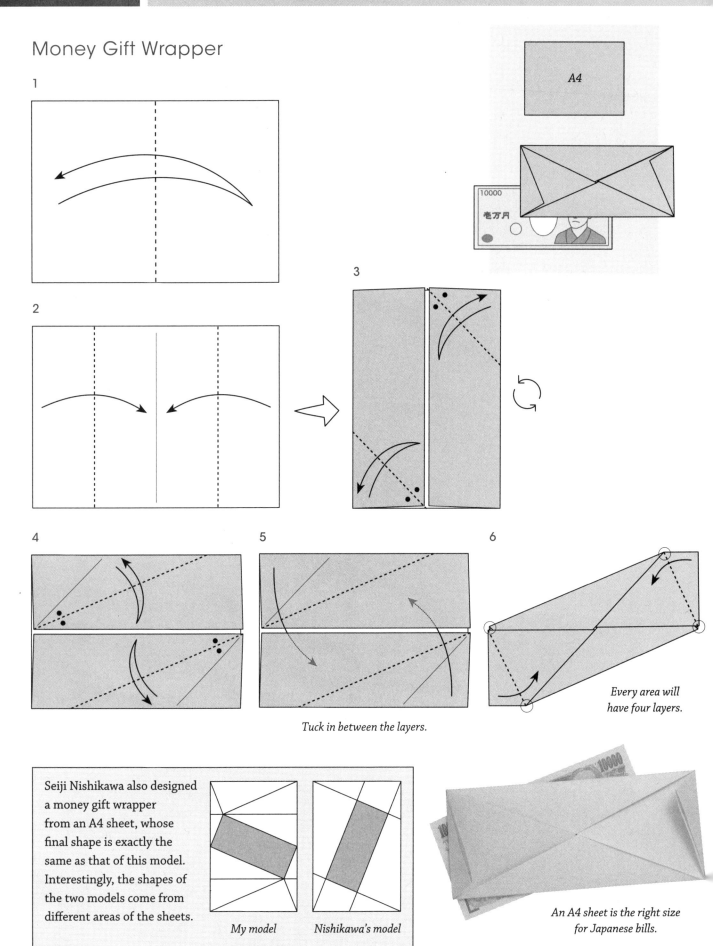

1

2

3

A4

4

5

6

Tuck in between the layers.

Every area will
have four layers.

Seiji Nishikawa also designed
a money gift wrapper
from an A4 sheet, whose
final shape is exactly the
same as that of this model.
Interestingly, the shapes of
the two models come from
different areas of the sheets.

My model   Nishikawa's model

An A4 sheet is the right size
for Japanese bills.

4. YIN YANG BOX AND POSTCARD TETRAHEDRON

Yin Yang Box

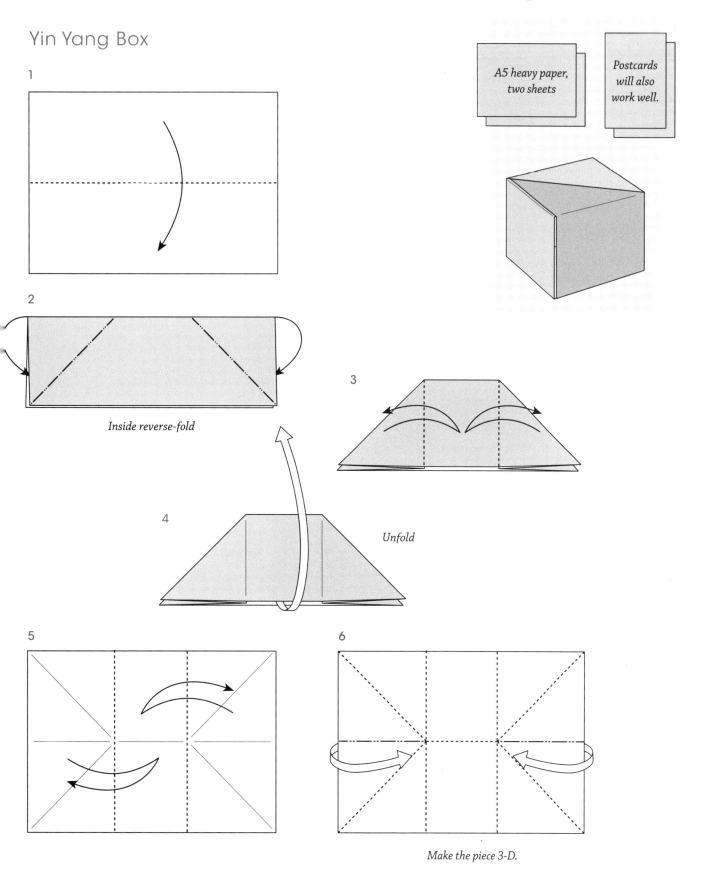

A5 heavy paper, two sheets

Postcards will also work well.

1

2

Inside reverse-fold

3

4

Unfold

5

6

Make the piece 3-D.

7

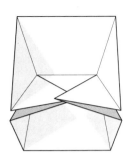

Make two pieces.

8

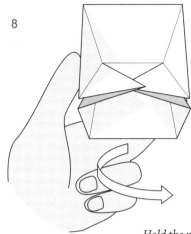 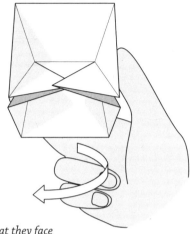

Hold the pieces so that they face toward each other, making sure the layers inside are mirror images.

9

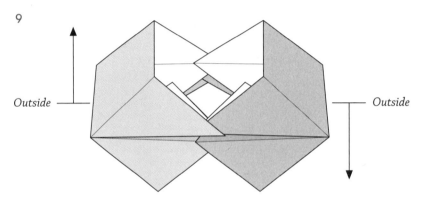

Outside ——   —— Outside

Assemble the pieces so that the top half of the left piece and the bottom half of the right piece will be outside.

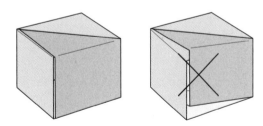

The model should not have an open slit.

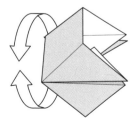

Twist gently while assembling if the pieces will not go smoothly. (You will not be able to assemble if you have the inside layers in a wrong position.)

ALMOST √2

As I mentioned earlier, we can use sheets with the aspect ratio "almost √2" for traditional models that are made of rectangle sheets. *Yin Yang Box* on page 21 is one of the few models included in the book that can be made of "almost √2" sheets. Such sheets have great potential as origami paper because we can apply the proportions in various ways as shown below.

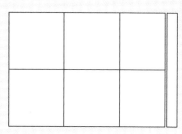

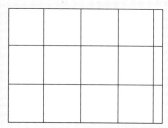

1 to 1 + α   *2 to 3 − α*   *3 to 4 + α*

Postcard Tetrahedron

JAPANESE POSTCARDS

The size of typical Japanese postcards is 100 x 148 mm, which was the size of the postcards issued by the government. I designed this tetrahedron according to the aspect ratio of the Japanese postcard. An A6 sheet, which is almost the same size, will be too short for the model.

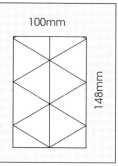

100mm

148mm

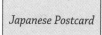
Japanese Postcard

1

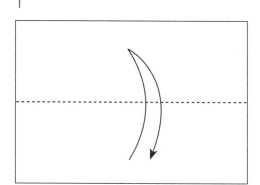

2

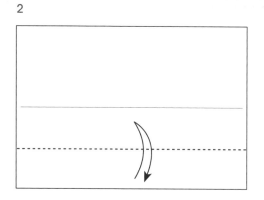

3

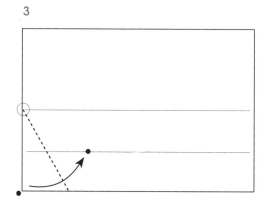

4

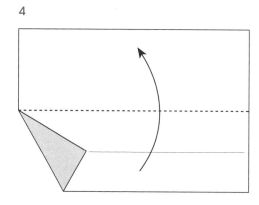

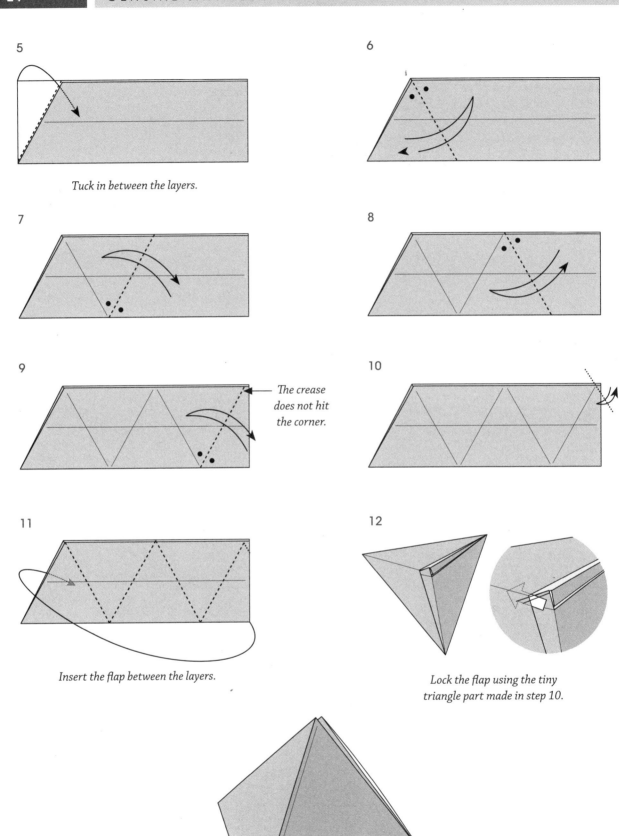

5

Tuck in between the layers.

6

7

8

9

The crease does not hit the corner.

10

11

Insert the flap between the layers.

12

Lock the flap using the tiny triangle part made in step 10.

5. HAT (TRADITIONAL) AND TRASH BIN

Use an A2 sheet to wear.

This hat is similar to the one depicted in an illustration for *Through the Looking Glass*, written by Lewis Carroll. You can use it as a trash bin by putting it upside-down.

This traditional model shows one of the properties of the silver rectangle.

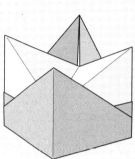

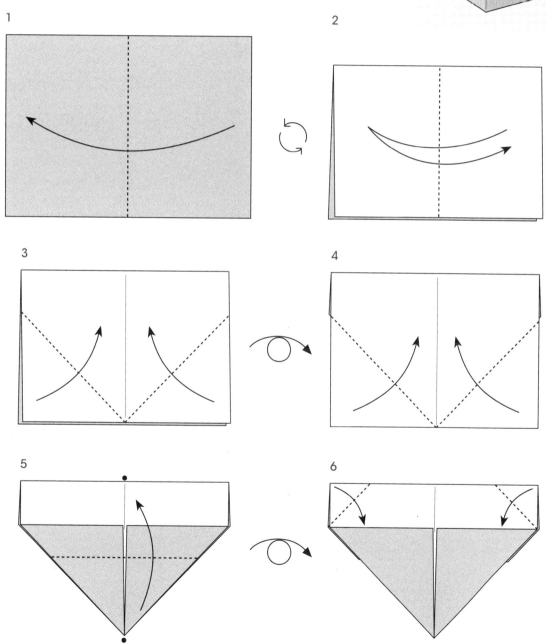

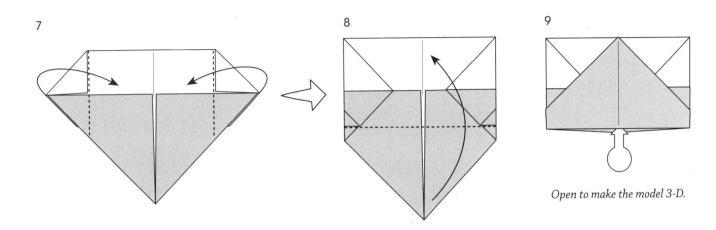

7   8   9

Open to make the model 3-D.

GEOMETRY OF THE TRADITIONAL HAT

Suppose you fold some creases in step 9 to make a square hat with its four points at the same height. Where do you need to fold? The answer is that you have to make two triangles on the top of the hat, each of which is the same as the triangle illustrated on the right. The triangle is a side of a square pyramid that comes out when one cuts a cube into six equal parts. The ratio of its height to its base is $1:\sqrt{2}$. I am going to utilize this property in many models presented in Chapter 3.

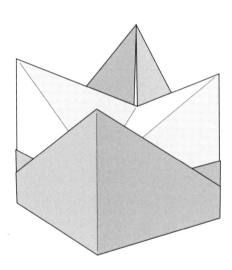

Trash Bin

This model is a geometry-oriented variation of the traditional hat. You can omit steps 5 to 10 and the insertion in step 11 to make the model in a hurry.

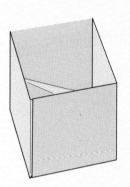

A4

1

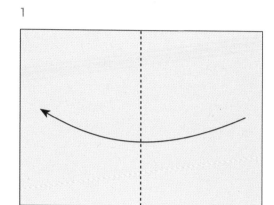

2

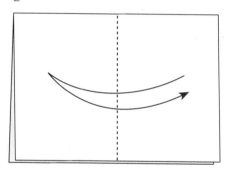

3

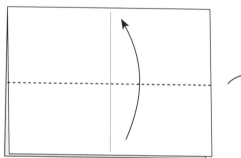

4

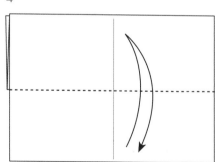

5

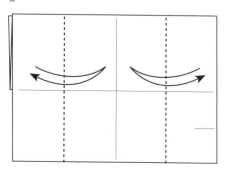

Pinch at the edge only.

6

7

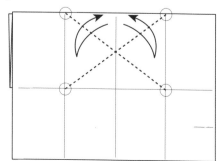

Fold the top two layers only.

8

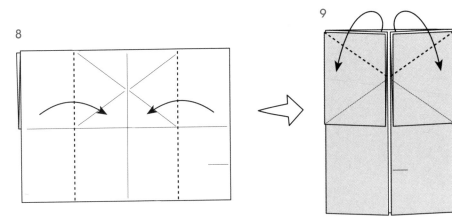

9

Fold two layers together along the creases on the layer below.

10

11

12

Open to make the model 3-D.

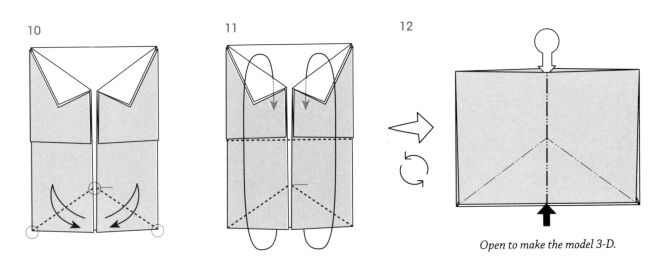

The outline of this model, indicated as the thin lines on the right, is a square prism whose volume is one half of a cube with the same height. Compare the figure with the one on page 26, i.e., six square pyramids in a cube, to understand the triangles inside of the model.

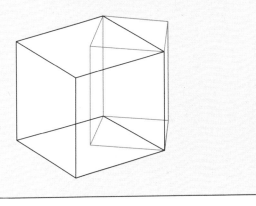

PROPERTIES OF THE SILVER RECTANGLE AND "MATCHING ANGLES"

ORIGAMI MODELS MADE FROM THE SILVER RECTANGLE

There are four properties of the silver rectangle origami:

(1) Utilizing matching angles of the silver rectangle

(2) Utilizing common rectangles as square + α

(3) Making models related to the cube using the proportions that appears in dividing a cube.

(4) Utilizing repeating patterns

They are often used in combination, but the models in chapter 2 will focus on (1), and those in chapter 3 will focus on (3).

22.5°

To conclude the chapter, I am going to elaborate on "matching angles." The matching angle of creases is specifically 22.5°, which is one fourth of the right angle. You have seen the angle when you check that your sheet is a silver rectangle as explained on page 17 (see the figure on the right).

The angle also appears in origami models made from the square, such as the Bird Base illustrated on the right.

So, when we fold silver rectangle sheets according to the angle that is one fourth of the right angle, we can treat the silver rectangle as, so to speak, a relative of the square and compose crease patterns that make points and edges meet each other.

Shown on the right is the most basic triangle in origami models folded according to 22.5°. The ratio of the lengths of the sides adjacent to the right angle is 1+√2:1, which equals the aspect ratio of the "remaining rectangle" when one removes a square from a silver rectangle. As I have said on page 15, the ratio itself is sometimes called the silver ratio.

Draw some lines at 22.5° in the triangle, and you can find the ratio 1:√2 everywhere, such as a:b, a+b:c, etc.

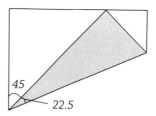

Folding a sheet to check that it is a silver rectangle.

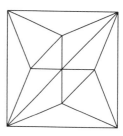

Bird Base

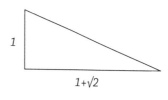

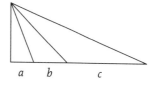

2 | √2 AND 22.5°

One quarter is just good.
The percentage of the lime for the cocktail Gimlet.

1. PLATE

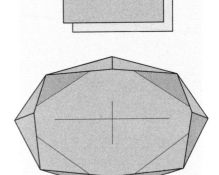

A4, two sheets

This is a practical model. I would call it "silver plate" as it is made from the silver rectangle.

1

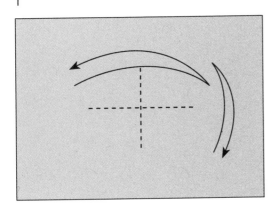

Fold about one third at the center.

2

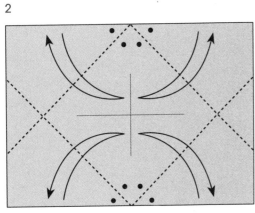

3

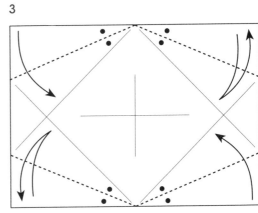

4

Stand up the edges to make the piece 3-D.

5

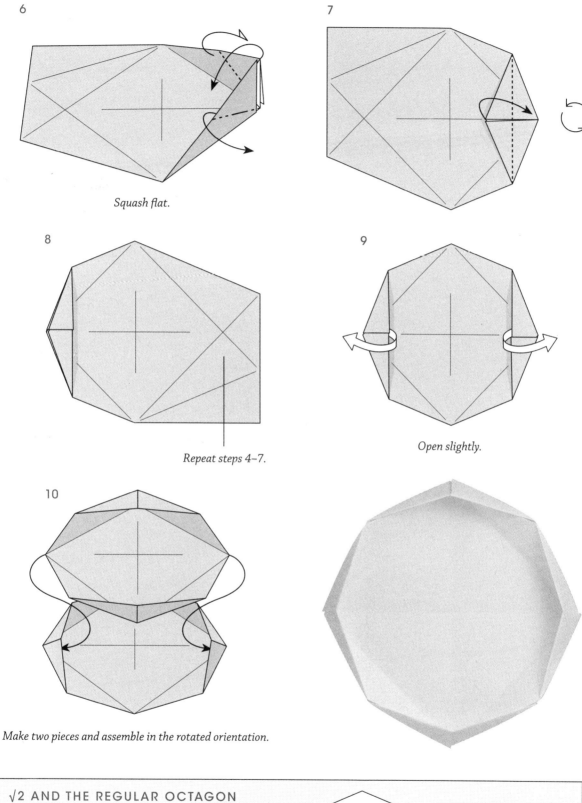

6

Squash flat.

7

8

Repeat steps 4–7.

9

Open slightly.

10

Make two pieces and assemble in the rotated orientation.

√2 AND THE REGULAR OCTAGON

√2 also appears everywhere in the regular octagon. The left figure shows the lengths of diagonals when the length of a side is 1. This model is based on the fact that the ratio of the longest diagonal to the shortest one is √2.

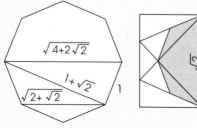

$\sqrt{4+2\sqrt{2}}$

$1+\sqrt{2}$

$\sqrt{2+\sqrt{2}}$

1

$\sqrt{2}$

1

1

2. OCTAGON WRAPPER

Here are two more models that exhibit the congeniality between the silver rectangle and the regular octagon.

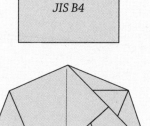

JIS B4

Octagon Wrapper 1

1

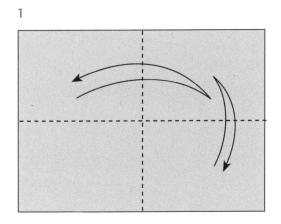

2

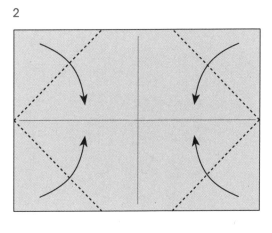

3

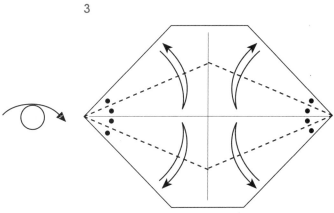

Fold the upper layer only.

4

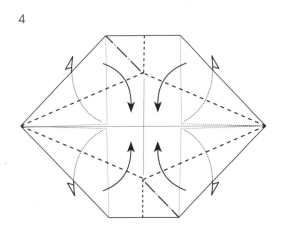

Rabbit-ear fold the upper layer only.

5

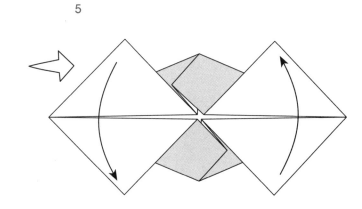

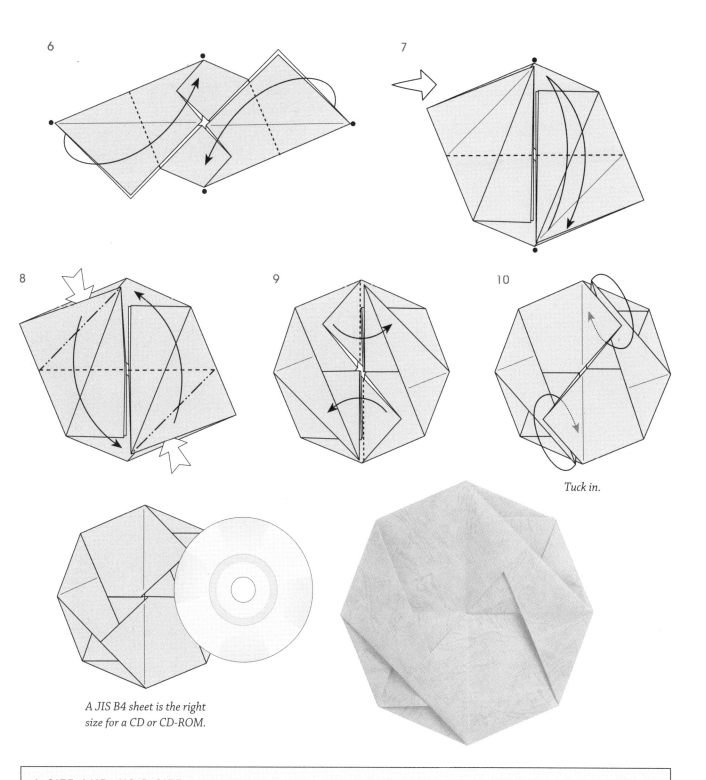

6

7

8

9

10

Tuck in.

A JIS B4 sheet is the right size for a CD or CD-ROM.

A SIZE AND JIS B SIZE

The regular octagons of these two models are almost the same size even though they are made in different ways. Then, how does the A series and JIS B series relate to each other? As I have explained on page 14, they are defined so that the area of A0 is 1.0 m^2 and that of JIS B0 is 1.5 m^2. The fact leads to an interesting geometric relationship. First, notice that the length of a side is $\sqrt{n}$ times longer when the area is n times larger (the length of a side of a square equals the square root of its area). Let the length of the longer side of an A size be $\sqrt{2}$, and the length of its diagonal is $\sqrt{3}$ by Pythagorean Theorem (see the figure on the next page). It is $\sqrt{3}/\sqrt{2}$ or $\sqrt{1.5}$ times longer than the length of the A size's longer side. That means the length of the longer side of a JIS B size is equal to that of the diagonal of the A size.

Octagon Wrapper 2

1

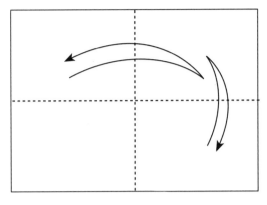

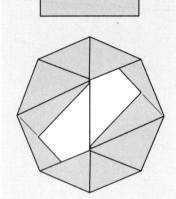

A4

2

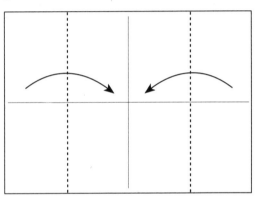

3

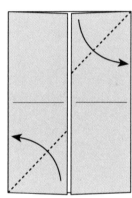

4

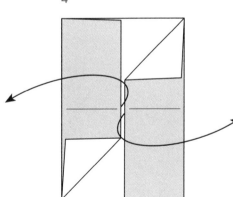

5

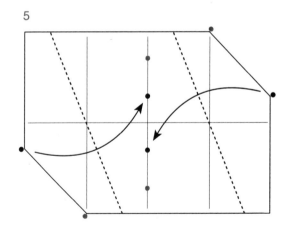

The length of the longer side of a JIS B size is equal to that of the diagonal of the A size.

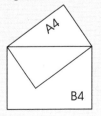

A4

B4

$\sqrt{3}$

1

$\sqrt{2}$

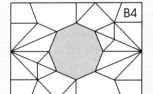

B4

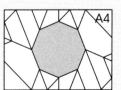

A4

These two regular octagons are almost in the same size because $(2-\sqrt{2})\times\sqrt{3}=1.014\,\mathrm{K}\approx1$.

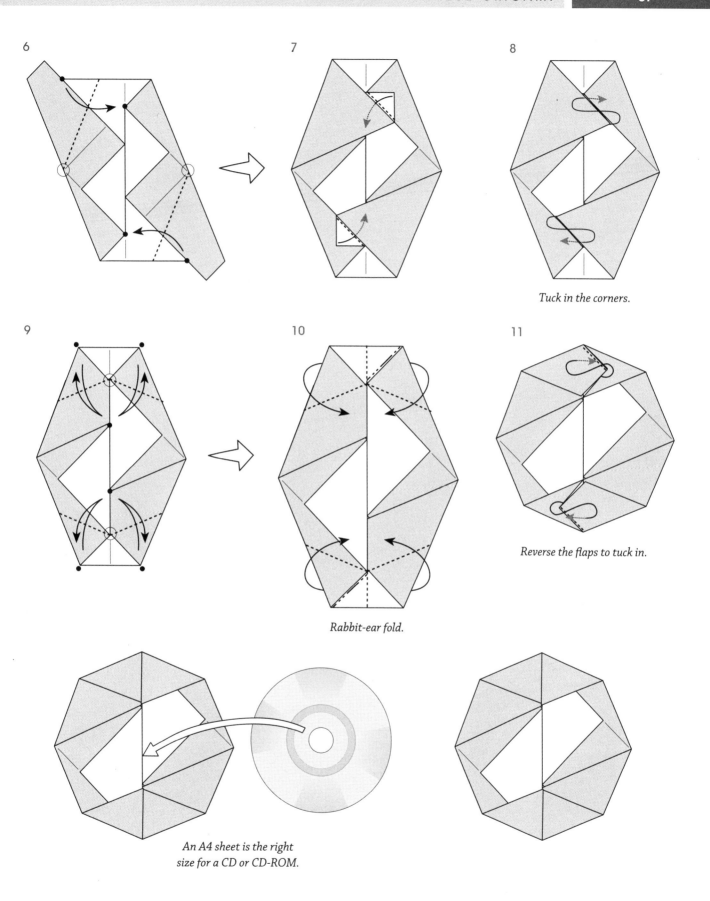

6

7

8

Tuck in the corners.

9

10

11

Reverse the flaps to tuck in.

Rabbit-ear fold.

An A4 sheet is the right
size for a CD or CD-ROM.

3. HEART-SHAPED WRAPPER

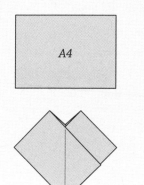

A4

I designed this model because the shape of step 4 reminded me of the heart shape in association with the bride.

1

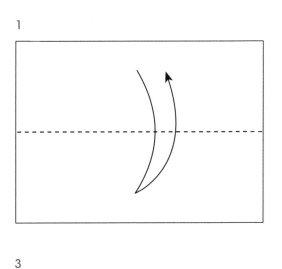

2

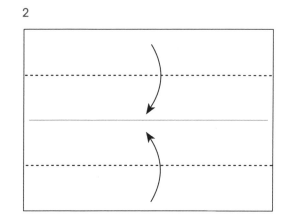

3

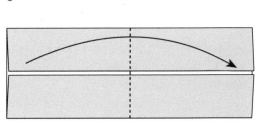

4

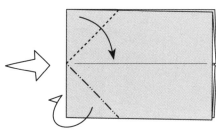

5

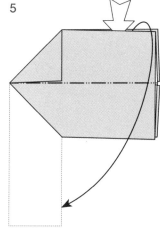

6

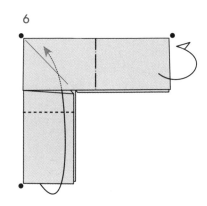

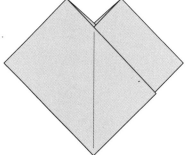

*Tuck in the corners on
both sides.*

3 GENUINE ORIGAMI³— √2 AND THE CUBE

Allen: [presenting a box] I got you something.

[Madison (mermaid) gazes at the box and kisses it.]

Madison: [without opening the box] It's beautiful. I love it.

Allen: No, you open it.

—from *Splash*, directed by Ron Howard

1. HONEYCOMB OCTAHEDRON

SHAPES DERIVED FROM THE CUBE

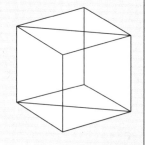

When you cut a cube (a regular hexahedron) through its opposite sides diagonally, you will have a silver rectangle section (see the figure on the right).

Then, what happens if you cut a cube into six square pyramids? (See the figure below.) A side of the pyramid is the triangle whose height is $\sqrt{2}/2$ times the base. Such a triangle rightly fits in a silver rectangle.

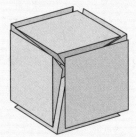

Hexasection of a cube.

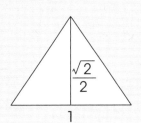

The ratio of the height and base of a side of the square pyramid that is one sixth of a cube.

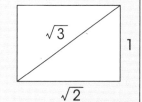

A silver rectangle in a cube.

If you flip the six square pyramids inside out, you will have an interesting solid. It, as a reversed cube, is called a rhombic dodecahedron because it is enclosed by twelve equal rhombi (see the figure on the right).

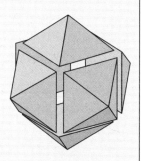

"Reversing" a cube.

HONEYCOMB OCTAHEDRON

The rhombic dodecahedron, as well as the cube, is one of the few solids that can tessellate the three-dimensional space by copying themselves like bricks.

If you combine two, instead of six, square pyramids that are one sixth of a cube, you will have an octahedron that is also space-filling. The outline of the models diagramed on pages 41 and 42 is this octahedron, though they have sunken faces. Hence I have titled them *Honeycomb Octahedron*. (Note that the name is not an accepted academic term.) Other space-filling solids include the 14-faced Kelvin's solid, which is enclosed by regular hexagons and squares besides the cube, the rhombic dodecahedron, and this octahedron. They play important roles in crystallography and other fields.

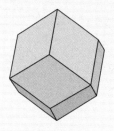

The rhombic dodecahedron.

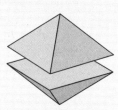

Octahedron that is two sixths of a cube.

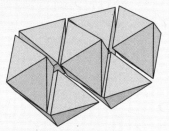

This octahedron is space-filling.

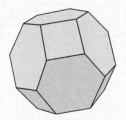

Another space-filling solid: the 14-faced Kelvin's solid.

Honeycomb Octahedron 1

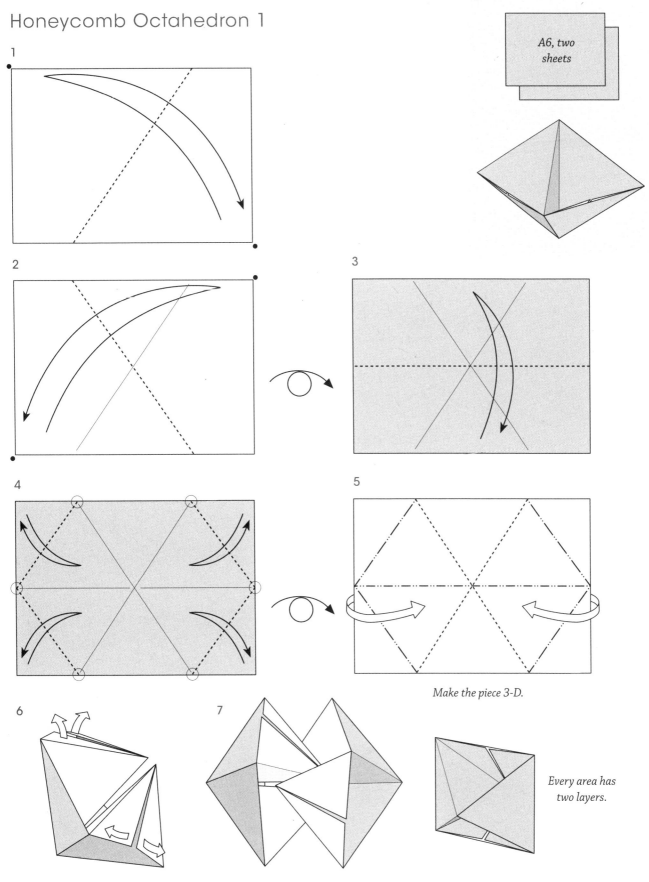

A6, two sheets

Make the piece 3-D.

Every area has two layers.

Lift up the raw corners so that they will "stick" on the faces of the other piece.

Make two pieces and assemble in the rotated position.

Honeycomb Octahedron 2

1

2

Pinch at the bottom only.

Two sheets

Remove a square from a silver rectangle.

3

4

Fold along the crease on the lower layer.

5

6

7

Make the piece 3-D.

8

Make two pieces and assemble.

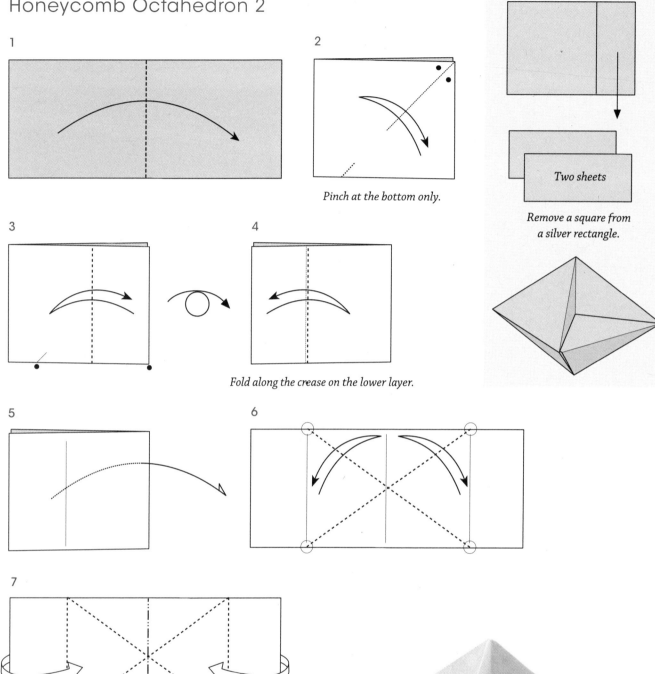
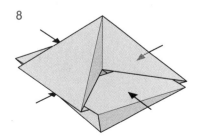

2. ONE-SHEET HONEYCOMB OCTAHEDRON

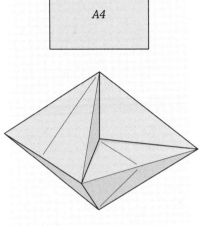

A4

1

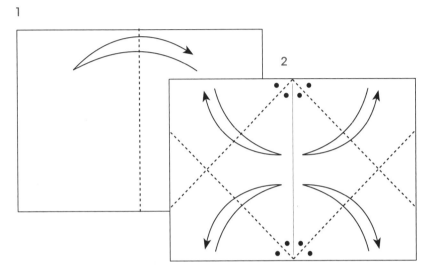

2

3

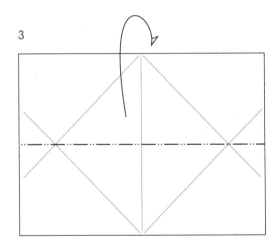

4

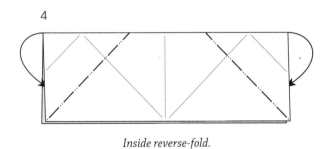

Inside reverse-fold.

5

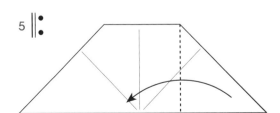

6

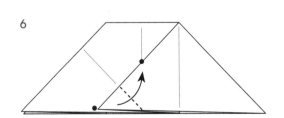

7

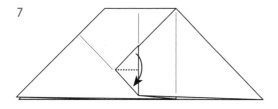

8

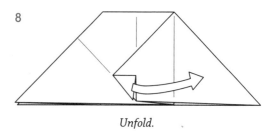

Unfold.

9

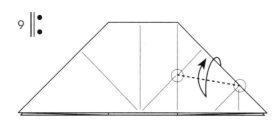

10

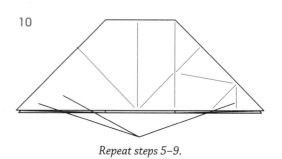

Repeat steps 5–9.

11

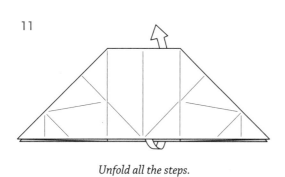

Unfold all the steps.

12

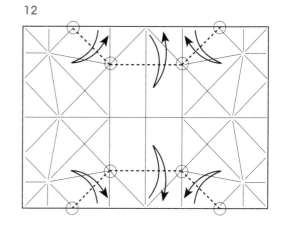

13

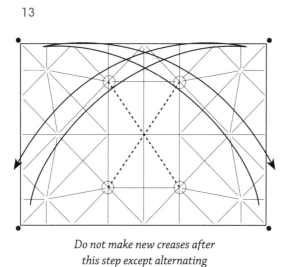

*Do not make new creases after
this step except alternating
mountains and valleys.*

14

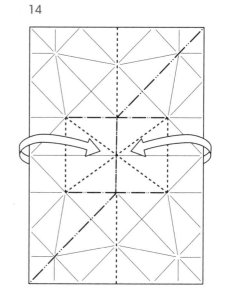

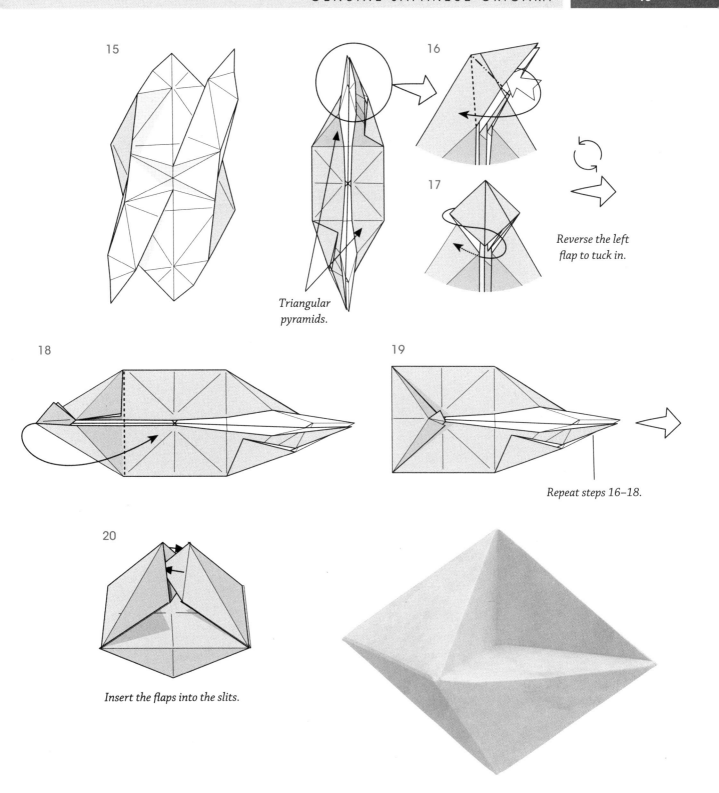

15

16

17

*Reverse the left
flap to tuck in.*

*Triangular
pyramids.*

18

19

Repeat steps 16–18.

20

Insert the flaps into the slits.

3. NON-SUNKEN HONEYCOMB OCTAHEDRON

A5, two sheets

You can make a pair of card holders with A7 sheets using the slits of the model.

1

2

3

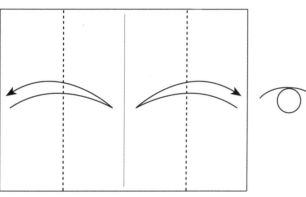
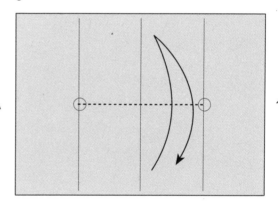

4

5

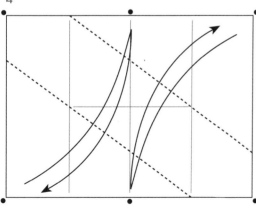
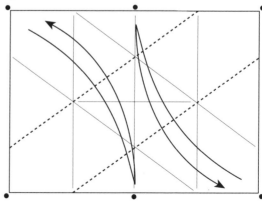

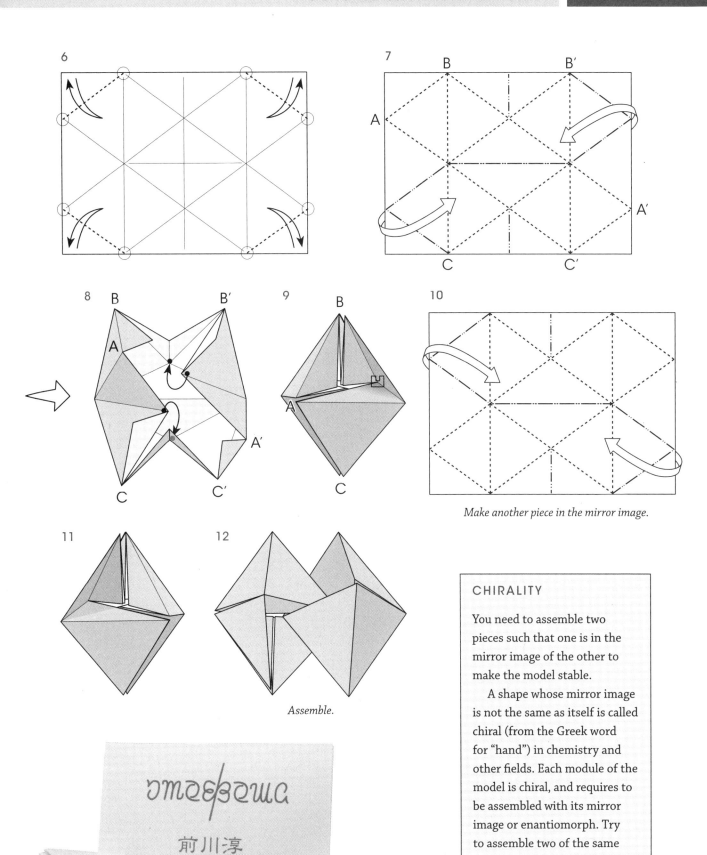

6

7

8

9

10

Make another piece in the mirror image.

11

12

Assemble.

おもてうら

前川淳

CHIRALITY

You need to assemble two pieces such that one is in the mirror image of the other to make the model stable.

A shape whose mirror image is not the same as itself is called chiral (from the Greek word for "hand") in chemistry and other fields. Each module of the model is chiral, and requires to be assembled with its mirror image or enantiomorph. Try to assemble two of the same modules and you will find the models will not be stable.

4. HONEYCOMB OCTAHEDRON IN COORDINATE SYSTEM

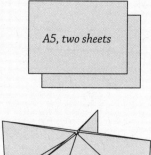

A5, two sheets

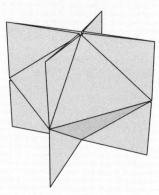

1

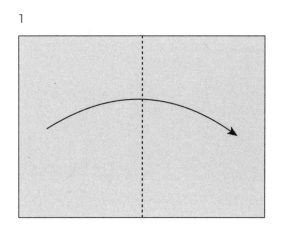

2

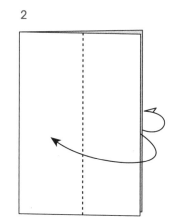

3

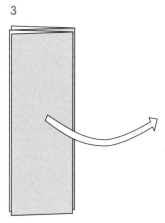

4

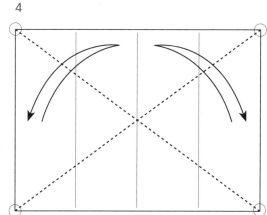

Fold firmly and precisely.

When you fold along a long line from one point to another, like step 4 of the model, scoring the crease with a ruler and an empty ballpoint pen may help.

5

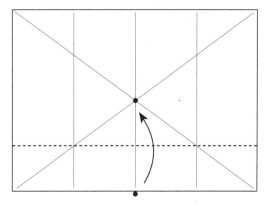

6

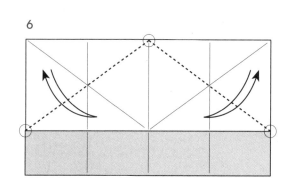

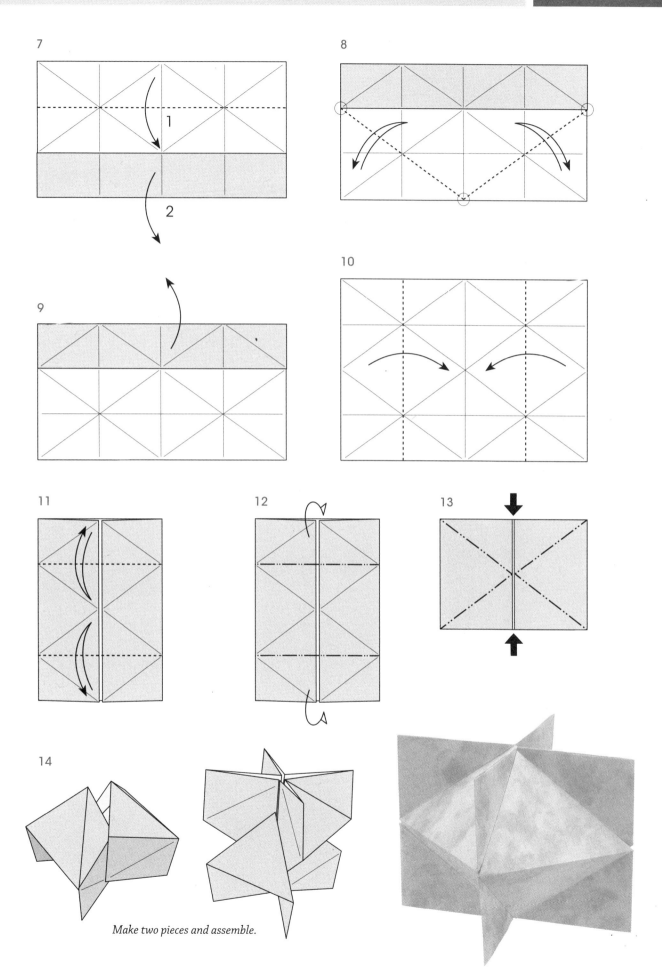

7

8

9

10

11

12

13

14

Make two pieces and assemble.

5. HONEYCOMB OCTAHEDRON IN INTERSECTING SQUARE PRISMS

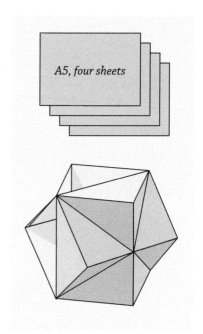

A5, four sheets

1

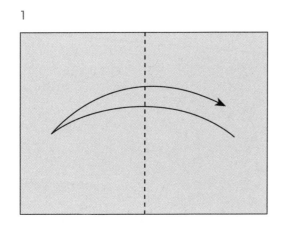

2

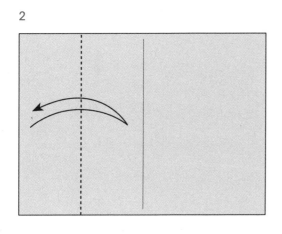

3

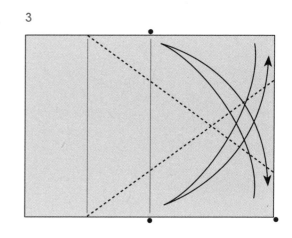

4

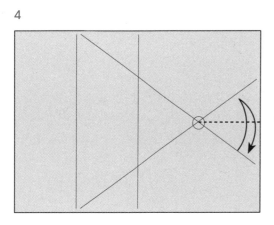

5

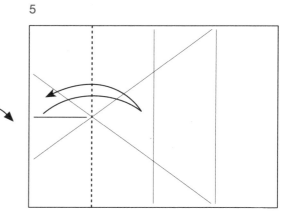

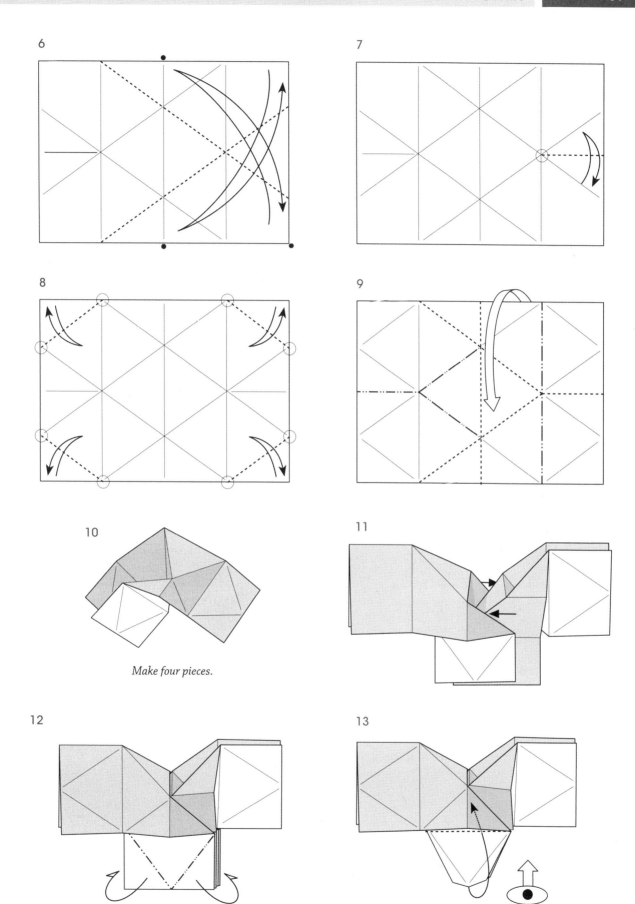

6

7

8

9

10

Make four pieces.

11

12

13

14

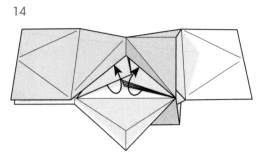

Align the flaps.

Repeat steps 11–14 to assemble all the pieces.

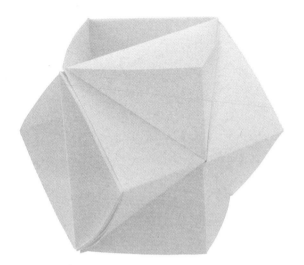

6. INVERTED CUBE

Rhombic Dodecahedron and Cube Skeleton

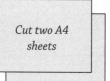

Cut two A4 sheets

You can make both *Rhombic Dodecahedron* and *Cube Skeleton* with the same modules by reversing them.

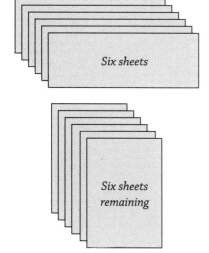

Six sheets

Six sheets remaining

Cut three silver rectangle sheets in half horizontally and another three vertically.

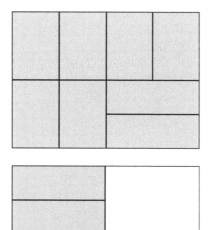

Cut this way, for example.

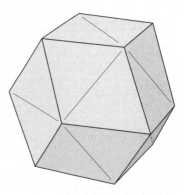

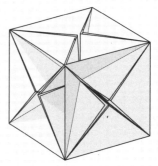

MODULE A

1

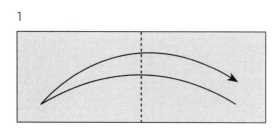

2

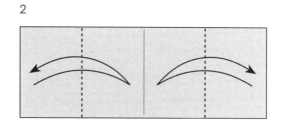

3

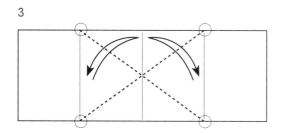

4

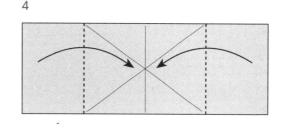

5

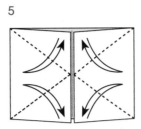
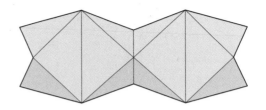

Fold along the creases on the lower layer.

Half-open to finish module A.
Make six pieces.

MODULE B

1   2   3

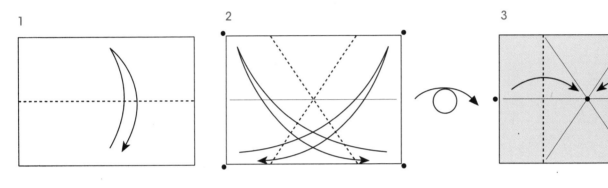

4   5

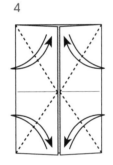
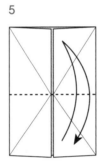

Fold along the creases
on the lower layer.

Half-open to finish module B.
Make six pieces.

Rhombic Dodecahedron

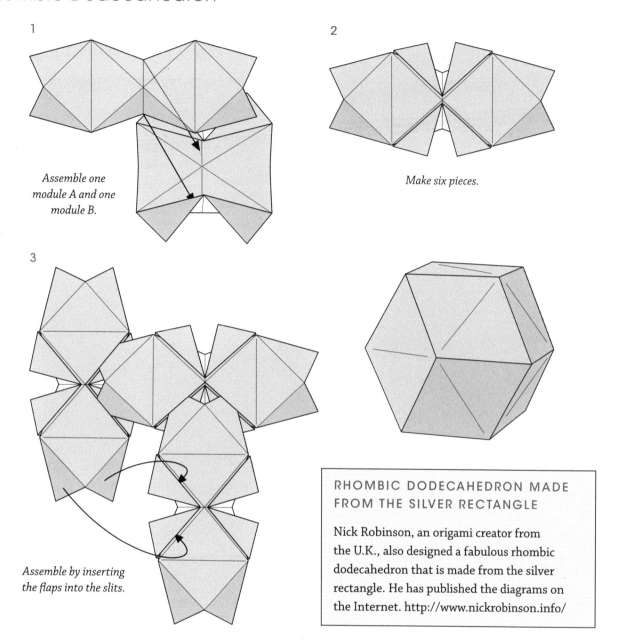

1

Assemble one module A and one module B.

2

Make six pieces.

3

Assemble by inserting the flaps into the slits.

RHOMBIC DODECAHEDRON MADE FROM THE SILVER RECTANGLE

Nick Robinson, an origami creator from the U.K., also designed a fabulous rhombic dodecahedron that is made from the silver rectangle. He has published the diagrams on the Internet. http://www.nickrobinson.info/

Cube Skeleton

1

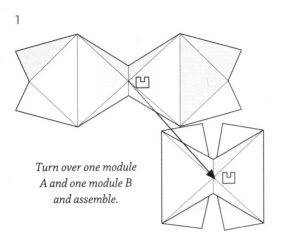

*Turn over one module
A and one module B
and assemble.*

2

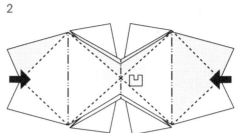

*Squash flat to
reinforce the creases.*

3

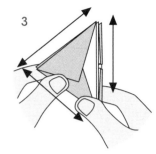

Reinforce the creases.

4

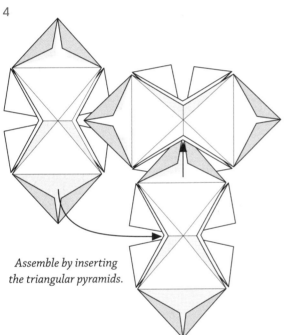

*Assemble by inserting
the triangular pyramids.*

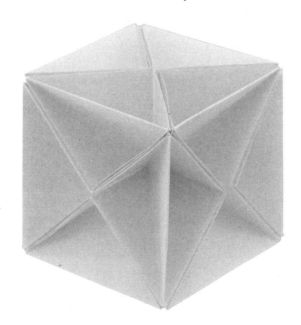

5

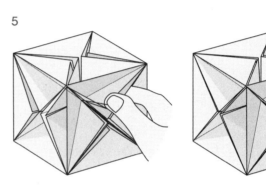

Align the flaps.

SIX SILVER RECTANGLES

Cube Skeleton can be seen as six intersecting silver
rectangles.

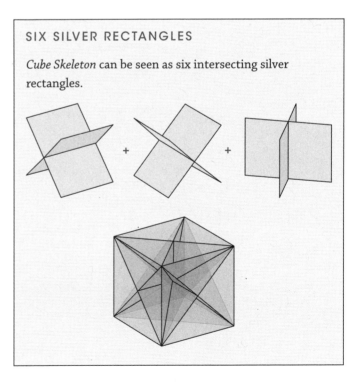

7. TWO-SHEET SUNKEN RHOMBIC DODECAHEDRON

Cut two
A4 sheets

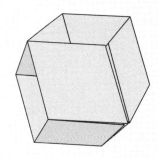

Make this model with a transparent plastic sheet to see its structure more clearly.

1

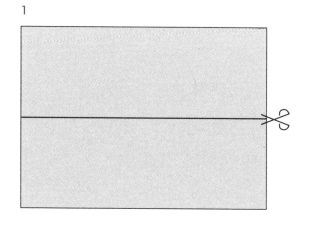

2

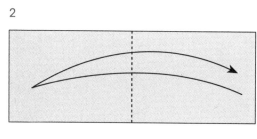

3

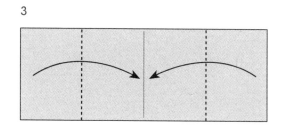

4

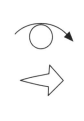

5

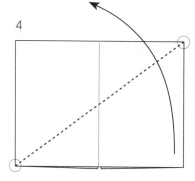

6

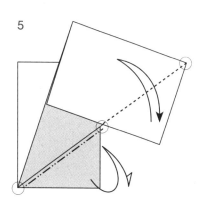

Unfold back to step 4.

7

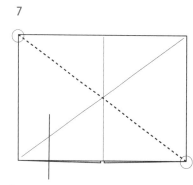

Repeat steps 4–6.

*After repeating,
unfold all the steps.*

8

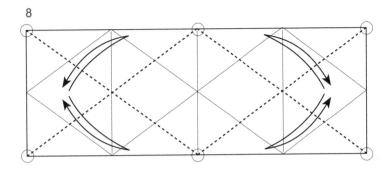

9

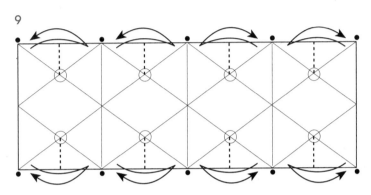

Do not fold inside of the rhombi.

10

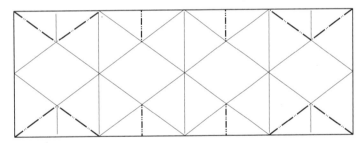

*Turn the twelve valley creases
into mountain.*

11

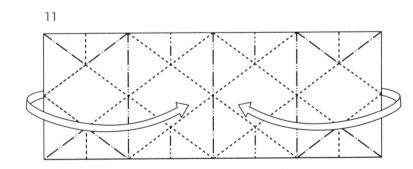

Make the piece 3-D.

12

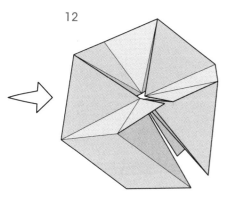

Make two pieces.

13

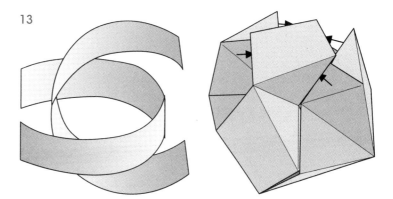

Assemble as illustrated by inserting the flaps into the slits.

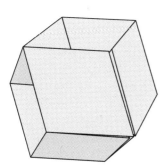

*Four of twelve faces should
be sunken to the center.*

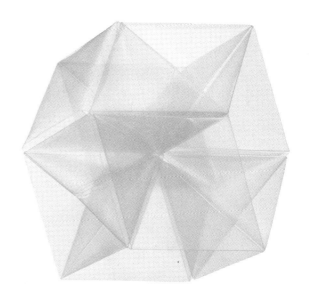

MARALDI ANGLE

The figure on the right shows the aspect ratio of a rhombic face of the rhombic dodecahedron. The larger angle is about 109.47 degrees.

The angle is called the Maraldi angle, named after the Italian astronomer Giacomo F. Maraldi (1665–1729). It is also the angle between two lines that connect the center and vertices of a regular tetrahedron. Maraldi found the angle in a rhombus at the closed end of a hexagonal column in the beehive and calculated its value. By the way, the rhombi in honeycomb were first discovered by the astronomer Johannes Kepler.

Four soap bubbles form the angle when they gather round, according to the law discovered by the physicist Joseph Plateau (1801–1883).

Honeycomb has the structure that saves wax the best, and soap bubbles take the structure that has the least area. These facts correspond to the most basic law in physics called "principle of least action," which says that movements and shapes can be explained as the phenomena that minimize a certain value. Most physical laws can be expressed in a form of the principle.

The Maraldi angle also appears in the diamond crystal. Carbon atoms bond each other to form the angle.

Aside from science, many rhombi in Japanese family emblems also have the angle, such as the most typical rhombic crest Takeda-bishi. The smaller angle is about 70.52 degrees, which is close to one fifth of 360 degrees (72 degrees).

about 109.47 degrees

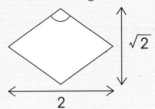

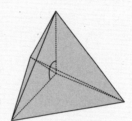

The Maraldi angle in a regular tetrahedron.

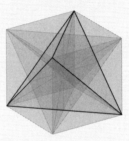

You can also find the Maraldi angle in the tetrahedron inscribed in the previous model Cube Skeleton.

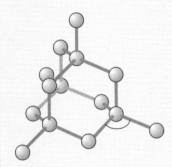

The Maraldi angle in the crystal structure of diamond.

Takeda-bishi, the crest of the Takeda clan, also has the Maraldi angle.

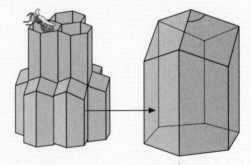

The Maraldi angle at the closed end of a honeycomb column. (The rhombus is the same as a face of the rhombic dodecahedron.)

8. SILVER TOWER

You should be able to make 1–2 m (3–6 ft) tall tower easily. Try to make it as tall as possible.

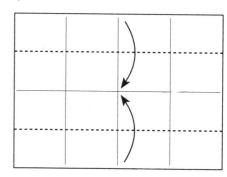

Cut two or more A4 sheets

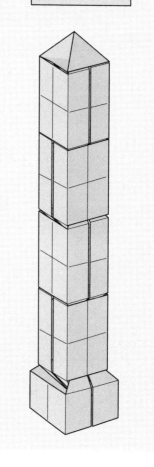

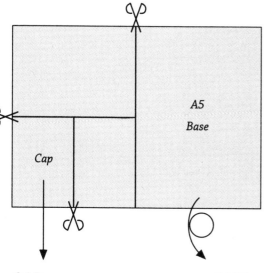

A5 Base

Cap

CAP

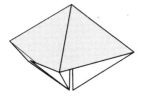

Make a module of *Honeycomb Octahedron* on page 40.

BASE

1

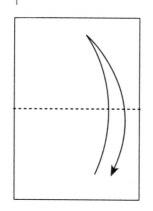

2

3

4

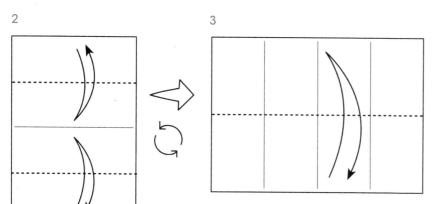

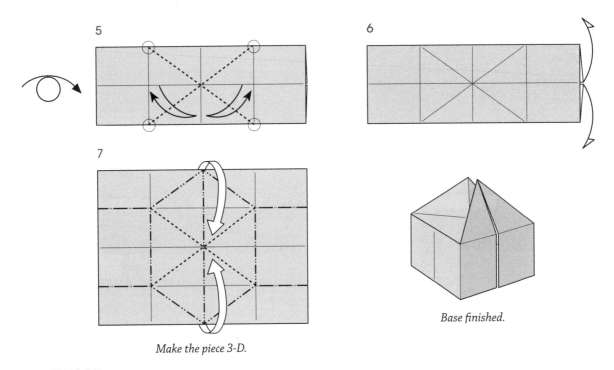

5

6

7

Make the piece 3-D.

Base finished.

FRAMEWORK

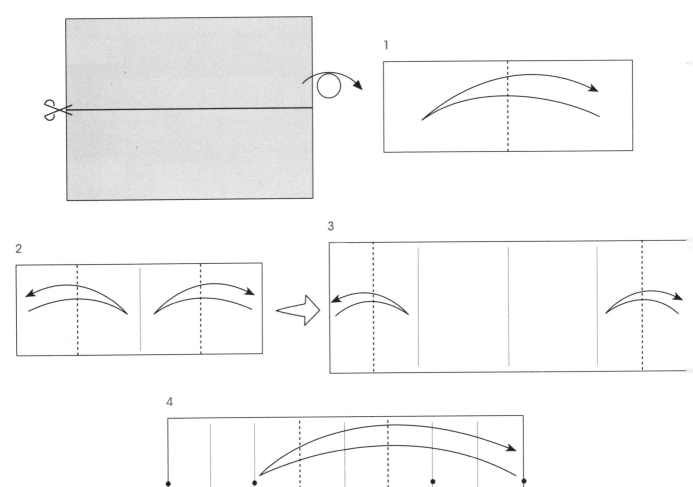

1

2

3

4

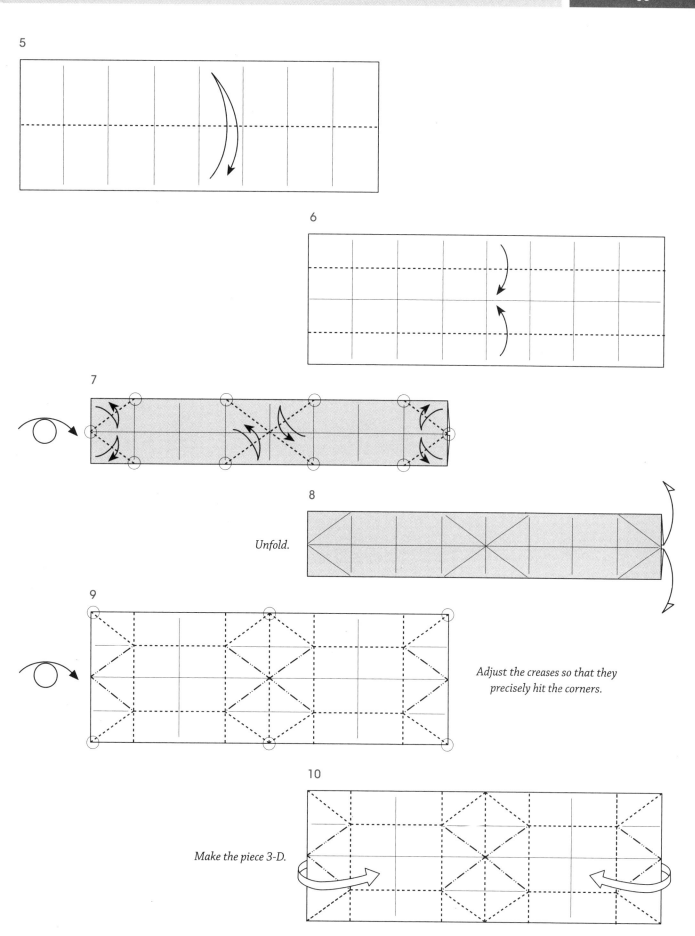

5

6

7

8

Unfold.

9

Adjust the creases so that they
precisely hit the corners.

10

Make the piece 3-D.

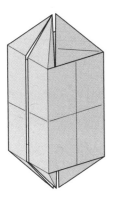

Framework finished.

Make several pieces.

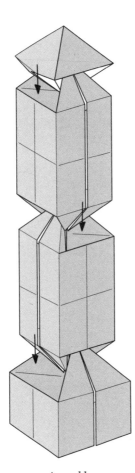

Assemble.

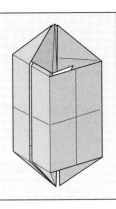

When using springy sheets close the open end of each framework by interlocking a cap piece (indicated as the gray part in the figure) in a rotationally symmetric way before assembling.

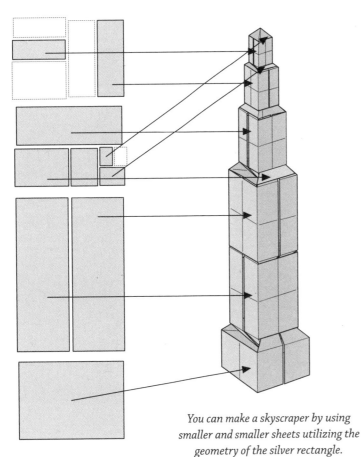

You can make a skyscraper by using smaller and smaller sheets utilizing the geometry of the silver rectangle.

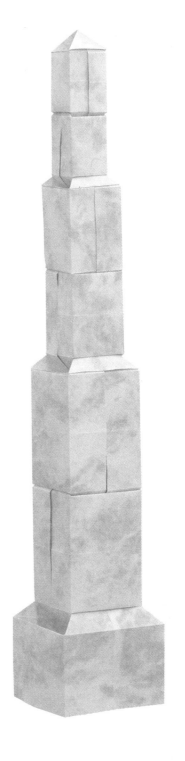

Plate (page 32)

Octagon Wrapper (page 34)

Money Gift Wrapper (page 20)

Yin Yang Box (page 21)

Trash Bin (page 27)

Box with Cat Ears (page 105)

Diagonally-Opening Gift Cube (page 107)

Box with Handles (page 109)

Cube Masu Box (page 111)

*Non-sunken Honeycomb
Octahedron (page 46)*

House (page 86)

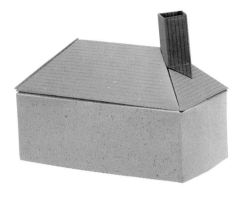

Hip Roof (page 98)

Re-roofing (page 90)

Silver Tower (page 61)

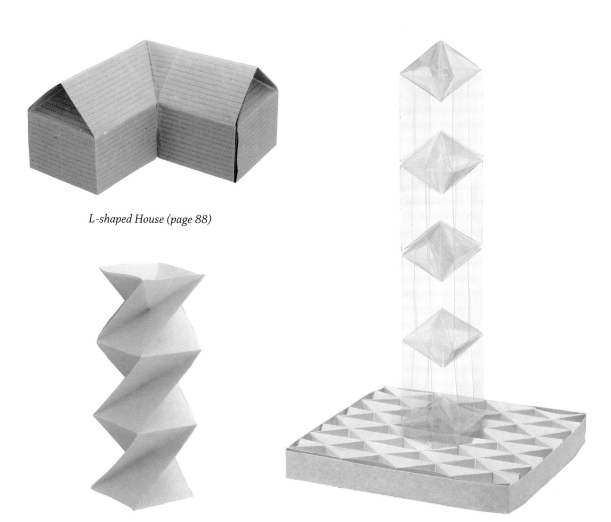

L-shaped House (page 88)

Triple Spiral Cube (page 69)

Silver Honeycomb (page 65)

Honeycomb Octahedron (page 40)

One-sheet Honeycomb Octahedron (page 43)

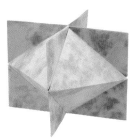

Honeycomb Octahedron in Coordinate System (page 48)

Honeycomb Octahedron in Intersecting Square Prisms (page 50)

Inverted Cube: Rhombic Dodecahedron and Cube Skeleton (page 53)

Two-sheet Sunken Rhombic Dodecahedron (page 57)

Loop Hole Cube (page 71)   *Half Z Cube (page 73)*

Plug-and-socket Puzzle Cube (page 76)   *One-third Cube (page 79)*   *Penta-hepta-hexahedron (page 102)*

Iso-area Half-cooked Cube (page 118)   *Hexa-roofed Polyhedron (page 83)*   *Cube Rose (page 114)*

The Die Is Split (page 123)   *Iso-area Hexa-cube (page 120)*

9. SILVER HONEYCOMB

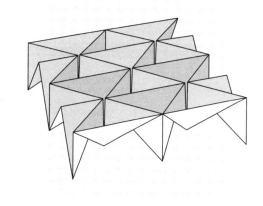

Cut an A4 sheet.

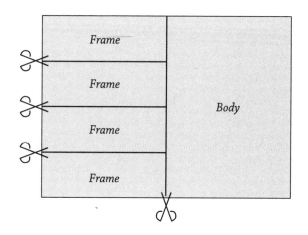

Body

1

2

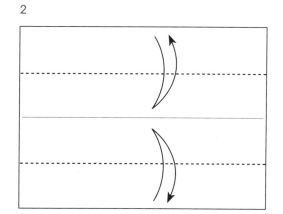

3

4

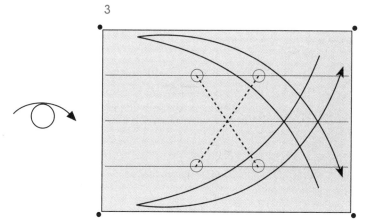

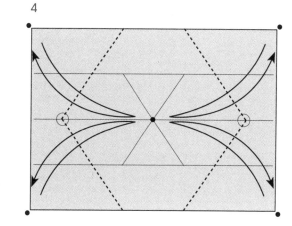

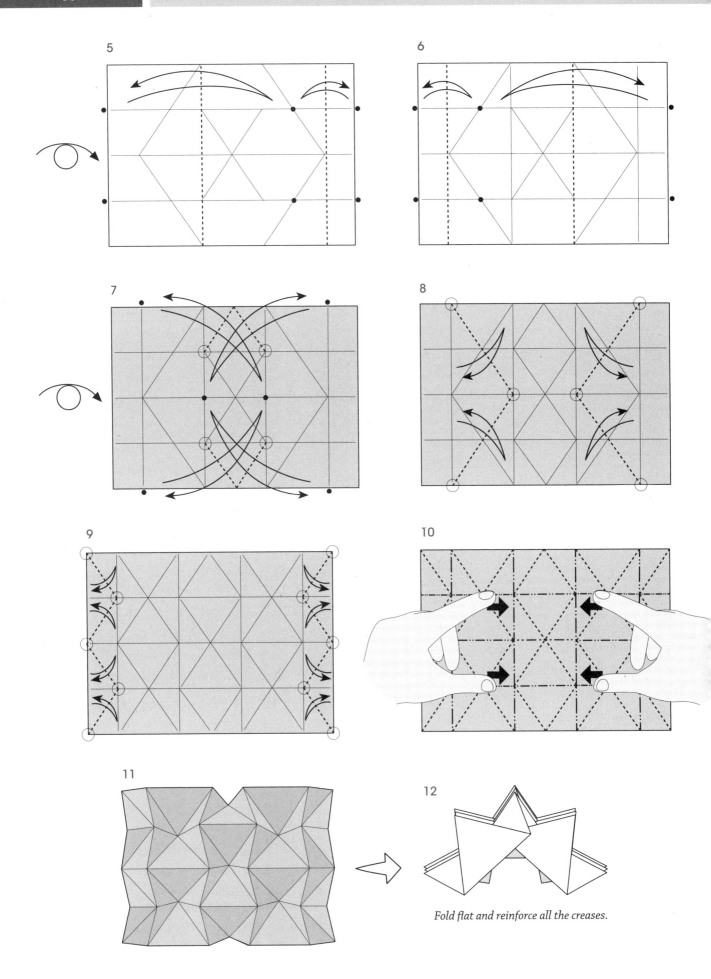

Fold flat and reinforce all the creases.

Frame

1

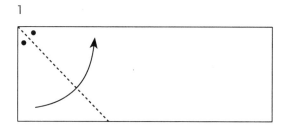

2

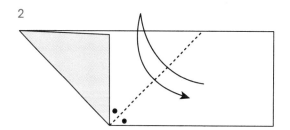

3

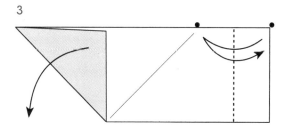

4

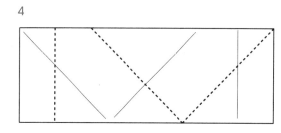

Repeat steps 1–3.

5

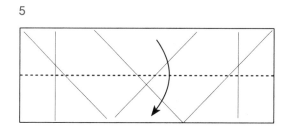

6

Make four pieces.

7

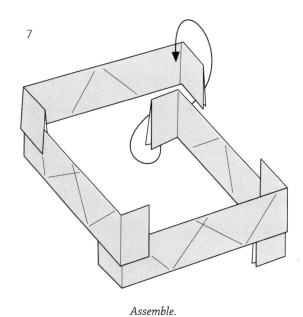

Assemble.

8

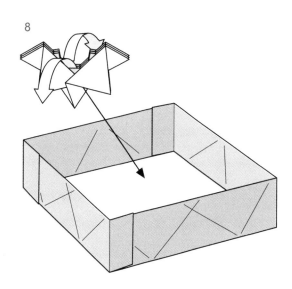

Open the body and fit it in the frame.

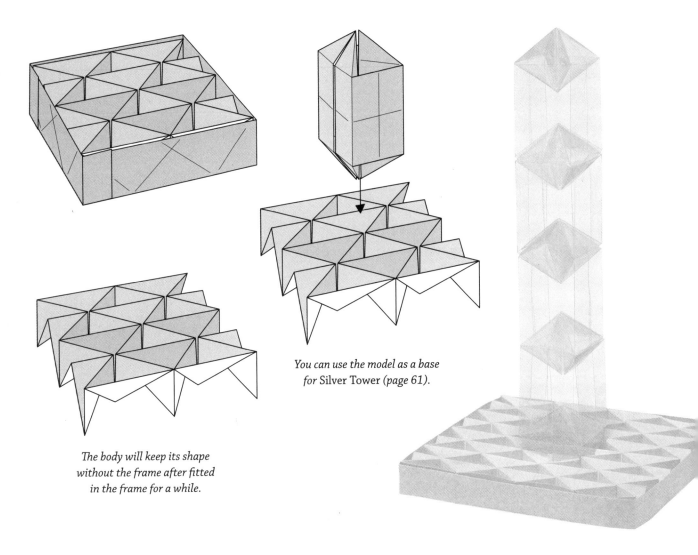

You can use the model as a base for Silver Tower *(page 61).*

The body will keep its shape without the frame after fitted in the frame for a while.

HONEYCOMB

The honeycomb mainly refers to the structure constructed from hexagonal prisms as seen in the beehive, and more generally refers to porous (having many hollows) repeating structures. It is used in airplanes and others that need strong, yet light, parts.

I have called this model "honeycomb" because it has the angle one half of the Maraldi angle (see page 60), which can be seen in the beehive. I do not think the pattern is used in industry.

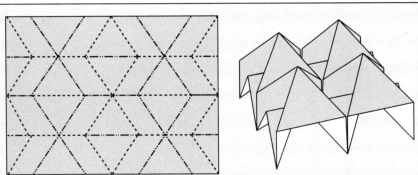

You can fold a finer pattern (see the photo above). You can also modify the pattern by changing the creases.

10. TRIPLE SPIRAL CUBE

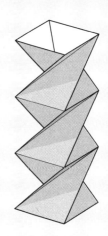

A4

The height of each tier is the same as the length of a side of the square end. That means each tier is inscribed in a cube.

1

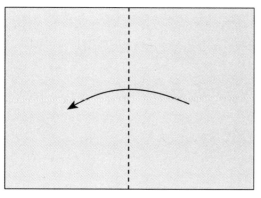

2

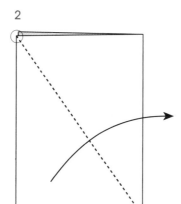

3

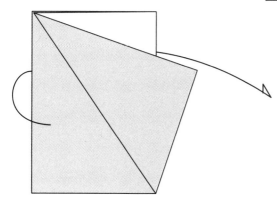

4

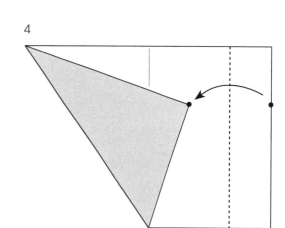

You have trisected the side in step 4, which can be proved using the facts that all the triangles in the figure below are similar and that the ratio of the sides is 1:√2:√3.

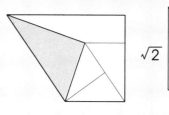

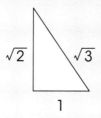

√2 √3

1

5

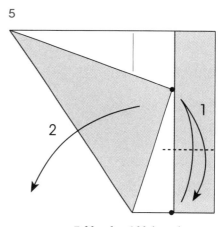

Fold and unfold the right half only, and unfold.

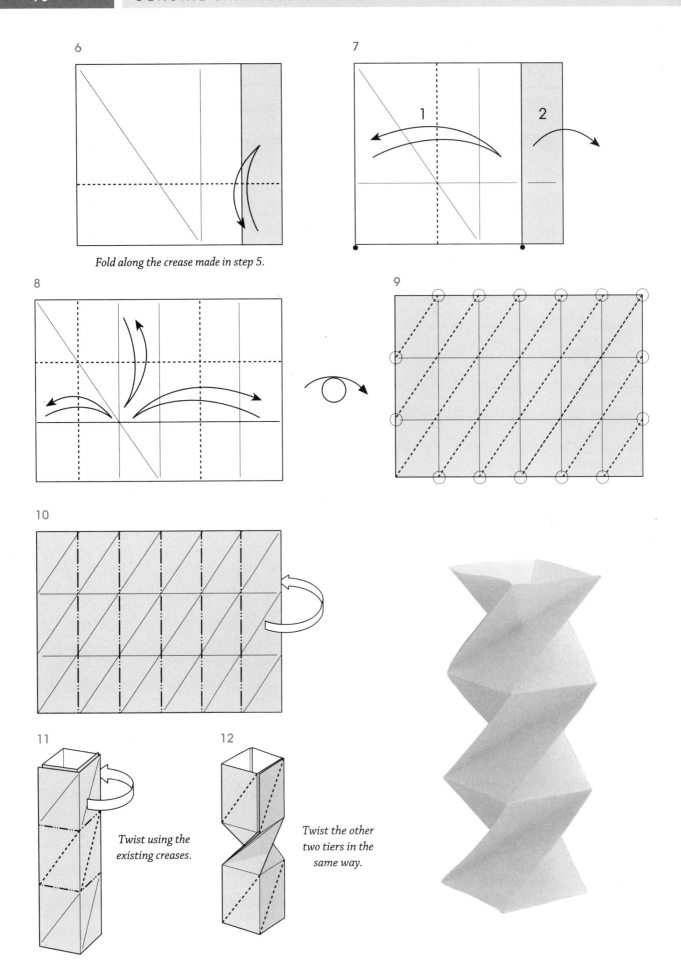

6

Fold along the crease made in step 5.

7

1

2

8

9

10

11

Twist using the existing creases.

12

Twist the other two tiers in the same way.

11. LOOP HOLE CUBE

I gave the model this title because it is basically a loop of a sheet and because it has a hole. I do not mean a cube with a loophole.

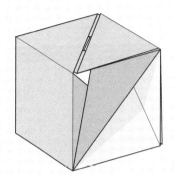

A4

1

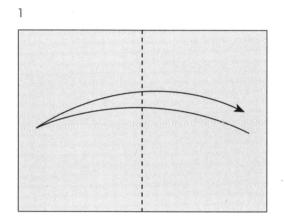

2

3

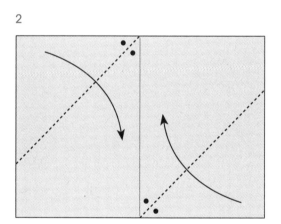

4

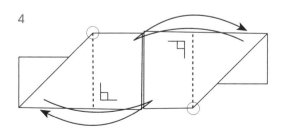

5

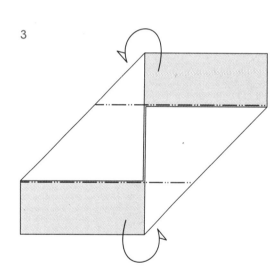

6

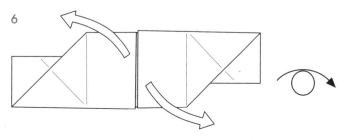

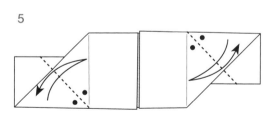

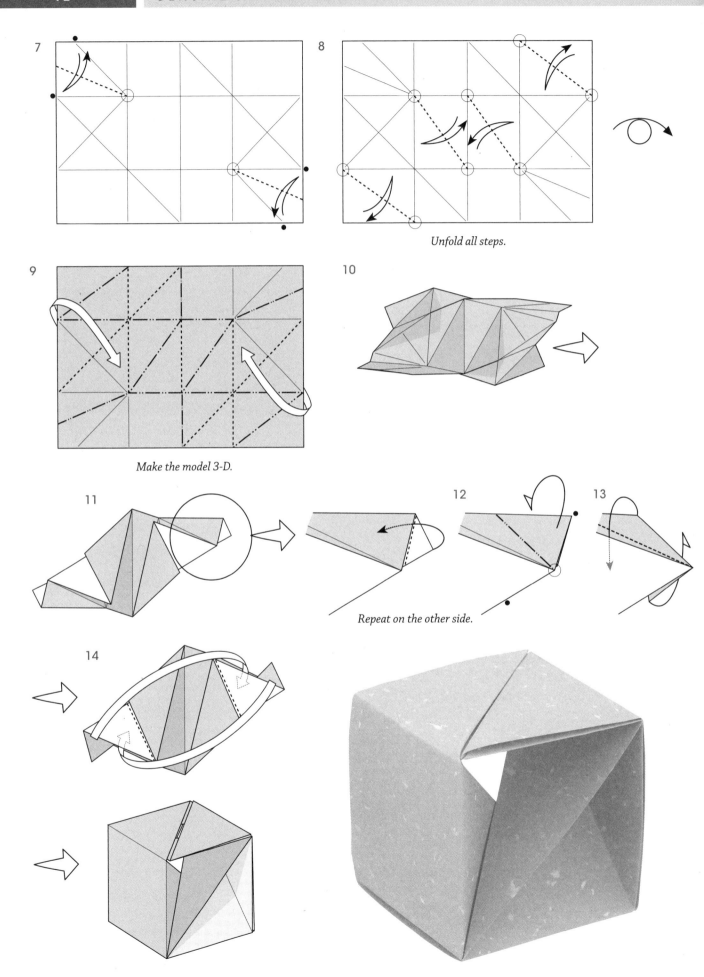

Unfold all steps.

Make the model 3-D.

Repeat on the other side.

12. HALF Z CUBE

A5

I have titled the model because it is one half of a cube and because it looks like the letter Z. The last step may be somewhat puzzling.

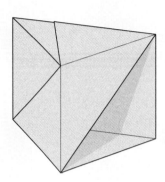

1

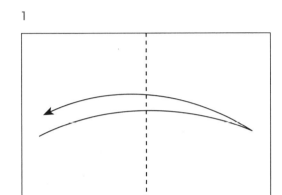

2

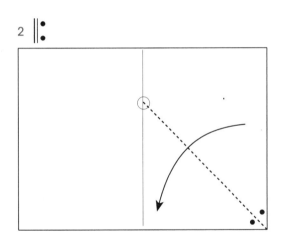

3

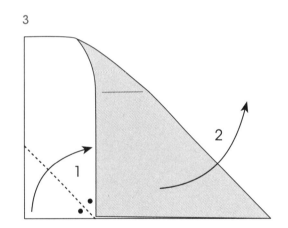

4

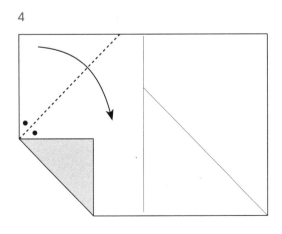

5

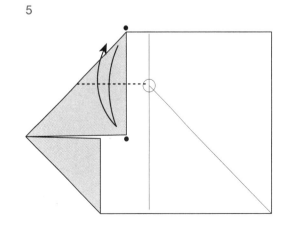

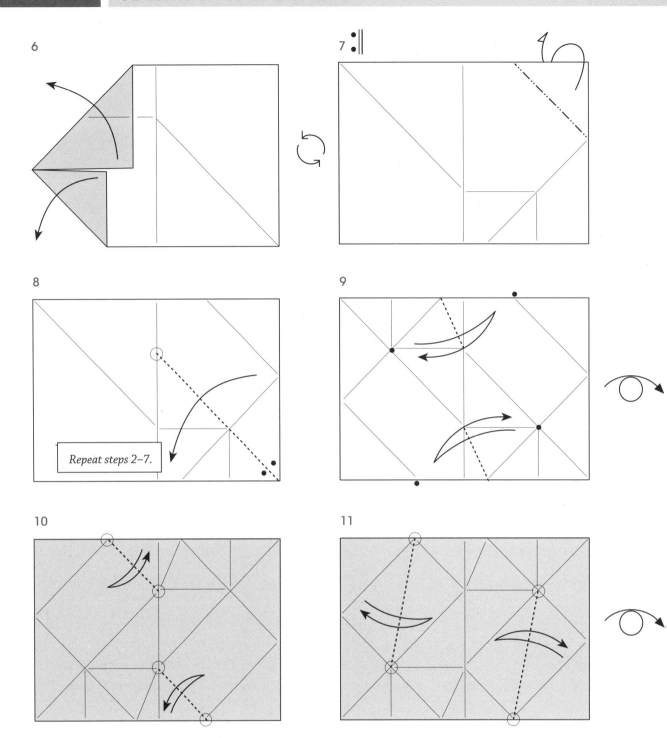

6

7

8

Repeat steps 2–7.

9

10

11

12

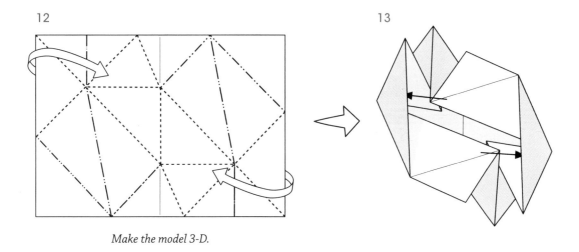

Make the model 3-D.

13

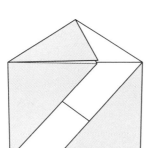

13. PLUG-AND-SOCKET PUZZLE CUBE

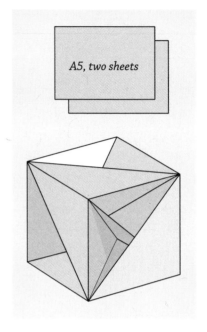

A5, two sheets

1

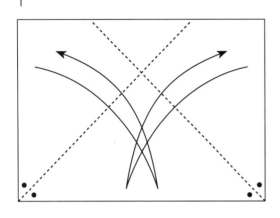

2

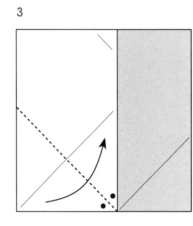

3

4

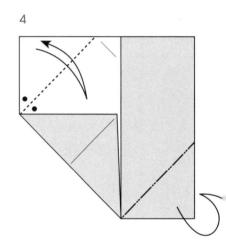

5

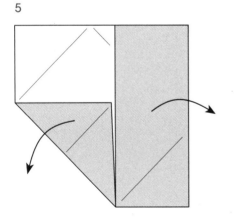

6

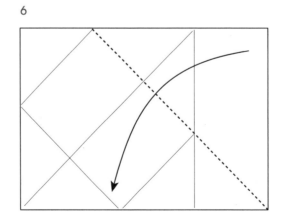

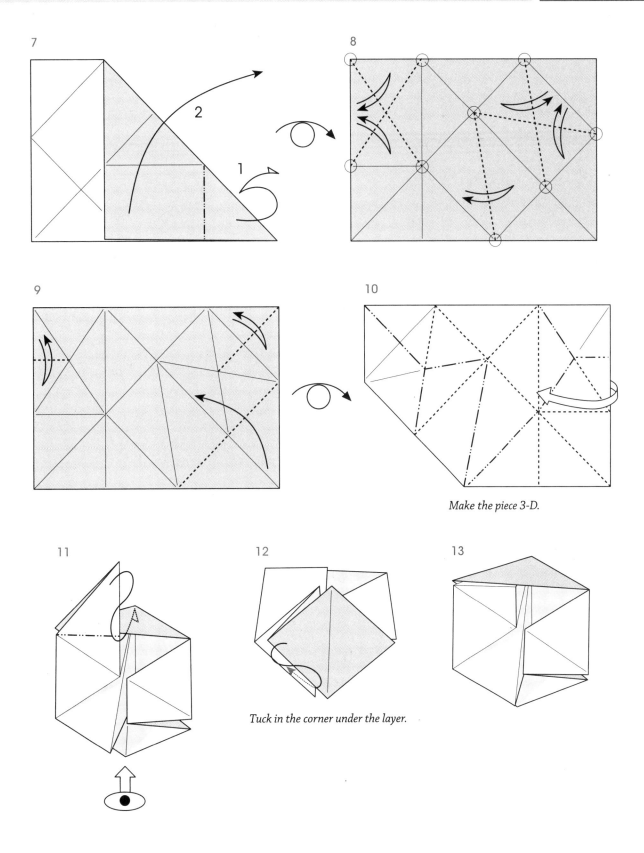

Make the piece 3-D.

Tuck in the corner under the layer.

14

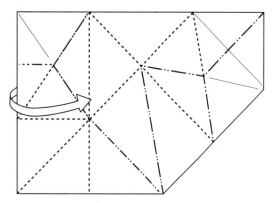

Make another piece in the mirror image.

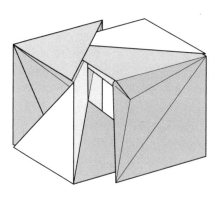

Enjoy as a puzzle.

14. ONE-THIRD CUBE

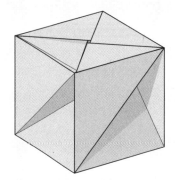

A4

The title comes from the fact that the model, as well as *Loop Hole Cube* on page 71 and *Half Z Cube* on page 73, has the volume that is one third of the cube.

1

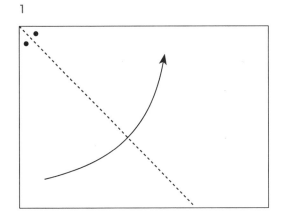

2

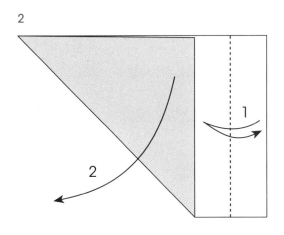

3

Repeat on the other side.

4

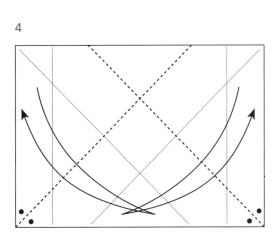

5

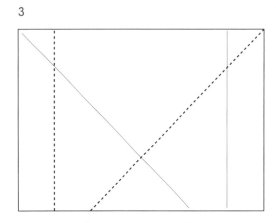

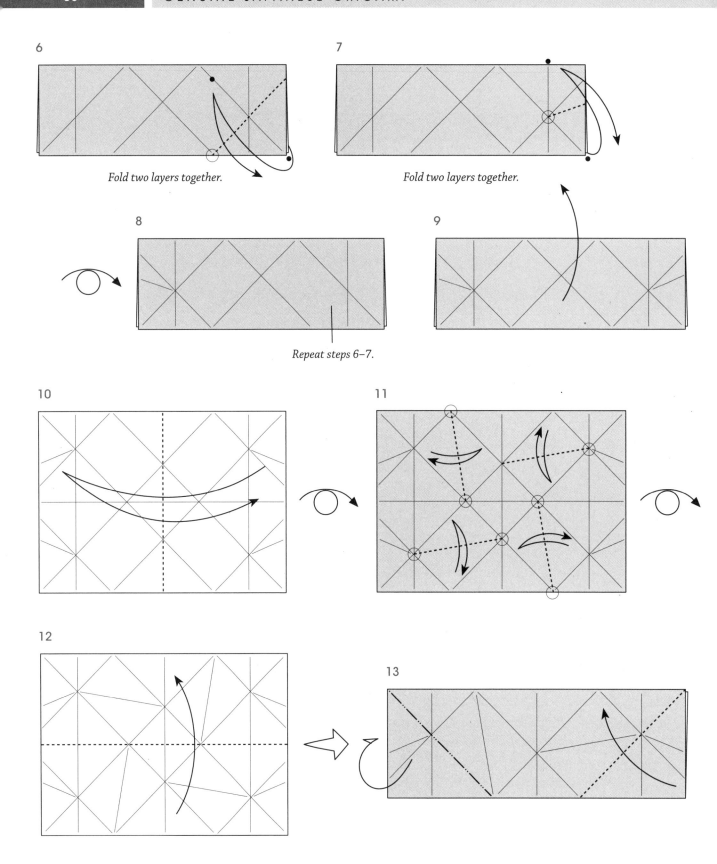

6

Fold two layers together.

7

Fold two layers together.

8

Repeat steps 6–7.

9

10

11

12

13

14

15

16

17

18

Insert the flaps.

Top view

Make trapezoid flaps using the existing creases and insert them into the opposite slits.

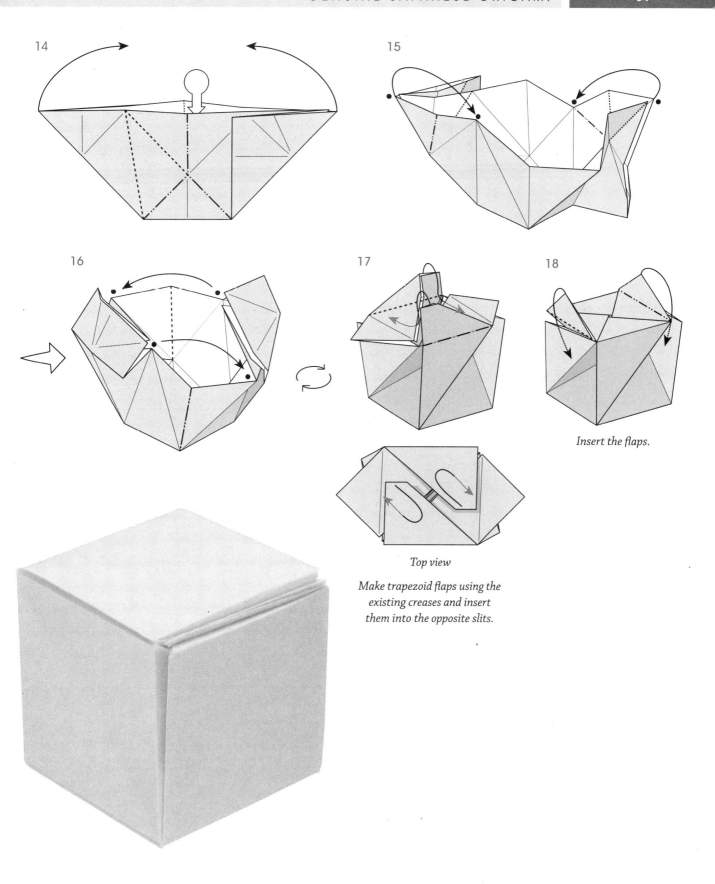

VOLUME OF A CONE

The area of a triangle is given by the formula "base times height divided by 2," but do you remember the formula that gives the volume of a cone or a pyramid? It is "area of base times height divided by 3."

Though you need some knowledge of infinitesimal calculus to prove the formula generally, examining this model may help understand the formula.

The volume of the model is one third of the cube because it encloses two square pyramid each of which is, as explained in the beginning of the chapter, one sixth of the cube (see the top figure on the right). You can confirm that using the formula. Because the pyramid has a square base and its height is one half of the side of the square, the formula gives 1 times 1 times 1/2 divided by 3, which surely equals 1/6.

Because its enclosed volume is 1/3, the total volume of its four holes, one at each side, is 2/3 of the cube, and the volume of each hole is 1/6. The formula also gives, as the base of the triangular prism is one half of the square, 1/2 times 1 divided by 3 equals 1/6. That means you can combine six triangular pyramids, three in the form and three in the mirror image or four in the form and two in the mirror image, to make a cube. I present the crease pattern for the pyramid on the right so that you can enjoy assembling as a puzzle.

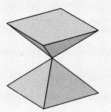

The volume enclosed by the model.

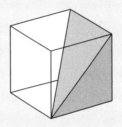

Each hole is a triangular pyramid that has the same volume as the square pyramid in the figure above.

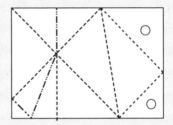

The crease pattern for the triangular pyramid that fills a hole. Tuck in the flaps indicated by the white circles to close the piece.

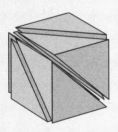

You can make a cube with six triangular pyramids that fill the holes (some are in the mirror image).

15. HEXA-ROOFED POLYHEDRON

I have named the model "hexa-roofed" because it is enclosed by six roofs. Its internal hollow is a rhombic dodecahedron.

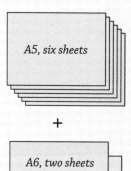

A5, six sheets

+

A6, two sheets (for internal support).

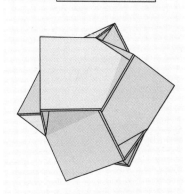

1

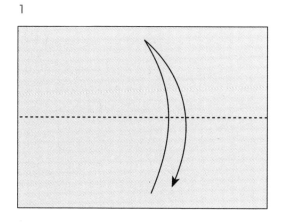

2

3

4

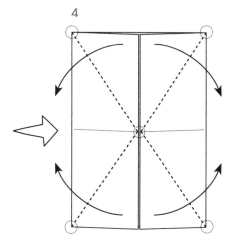

5

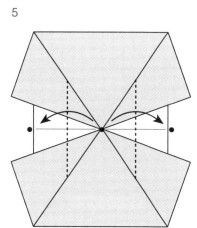

6

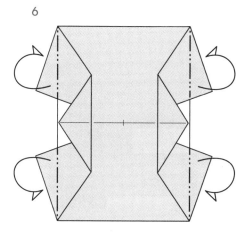

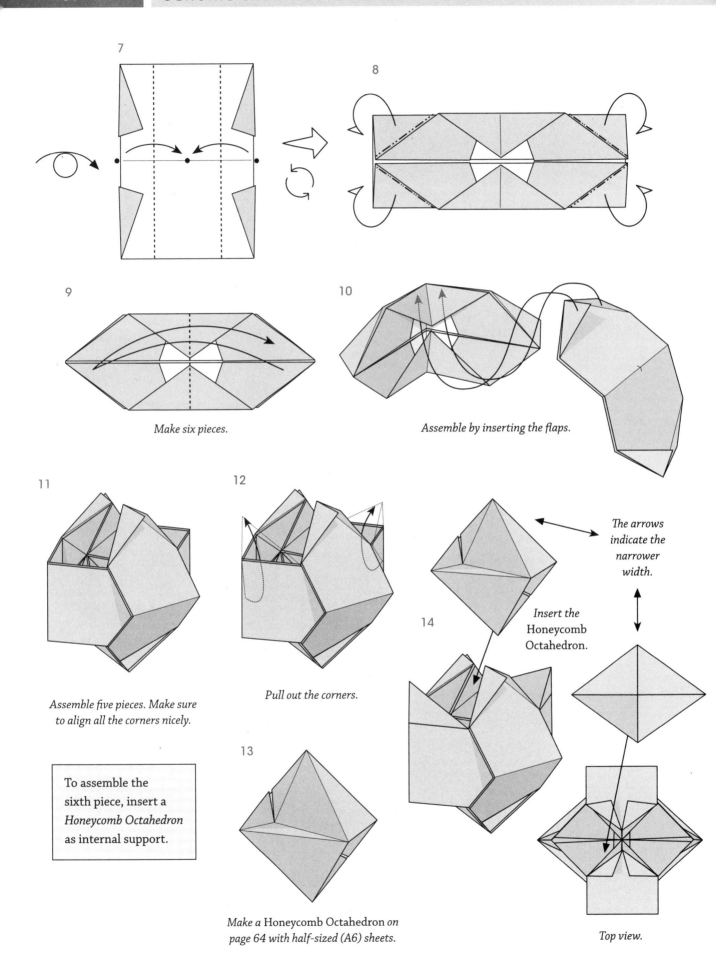

7

8

9

Make six pieces.

10

Assemble by inserting the flaps.

11

Assemble five pieces. Make sure
to align all the corners nicely.

12

Pull out the corners.

To assemble the
sixth piece, insert a
Honeycomb Octahedron
as internal support.

13

Make a Honeycomb Octahedron on
page 64 with half-sized (A6) sheets.

14

The arrows
indicate the
narrower
width.

Insert the
Honeycomb
Octahedron.

Top view.

15

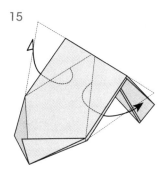

Pull out the corners.

16

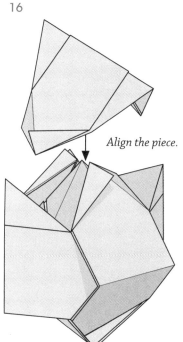

Align the piece.

17

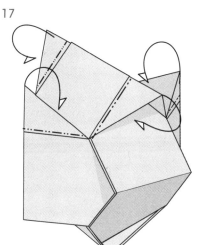

Fold the corners over the layers.

HEXA-ROOFED POLYHEDRON 2

Here is the crease pattern for a variation of the model that does not have sunken faces. Assemble six sheets. Its internal hollow is a cube.

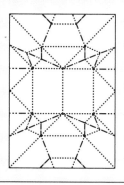

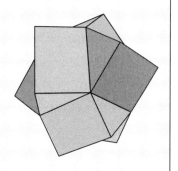

RHOMBIC DODECAHEDRON AND SQUARE PRISMS

This model demonstrates the fact that the rhombic dodecahedron is the intersection of three square prisms.

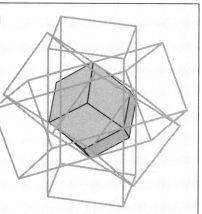

16. HOUSE

It is fun to make the model with a real estate flyer. It is one of my favorite models in the book.

A4

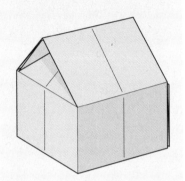

1

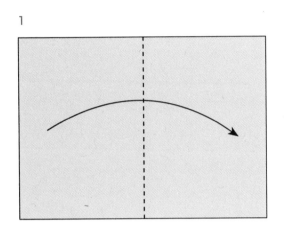

2

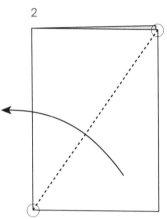

3

4

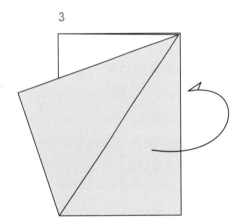

5

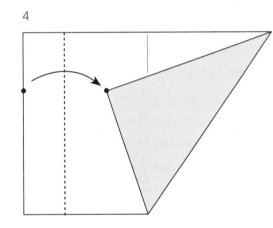

6

7

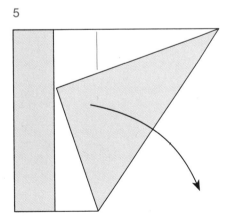

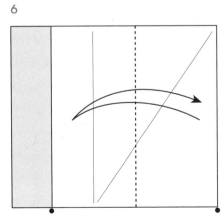

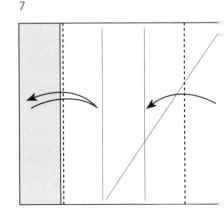

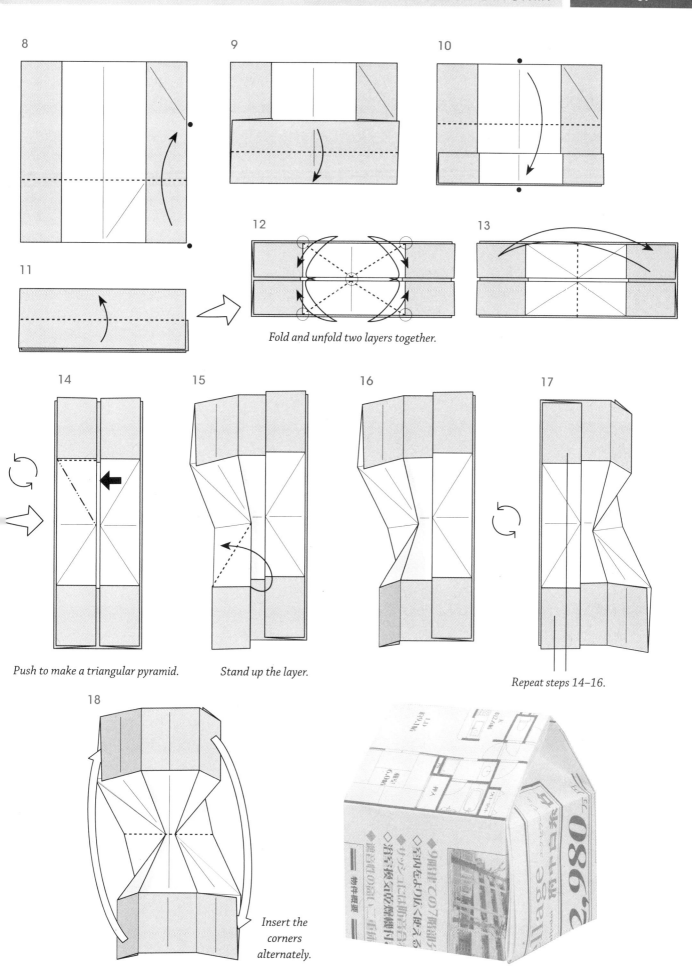

8

9

10

11

12

Fold and unfold two layers together.

13

14

Push to make a triangular pyramid.

15

Stand up the layer.

16

17

Repeat steps 14–16.

18

Insert the corners alternately.

17. L-SHAPED HOUSE

This architectural style is typical of the Tono area, Iwate in the northern part of Japan. Such a house contains stables in it.

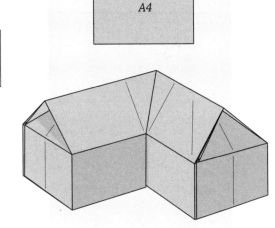

1

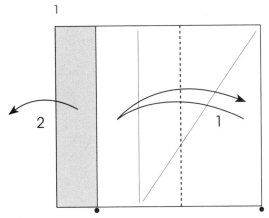

Start from step 6 of House *on page 86.*

2

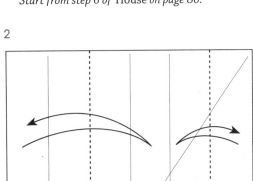

3

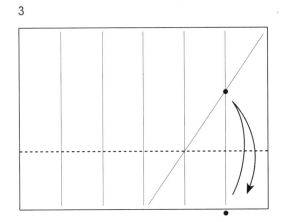

4

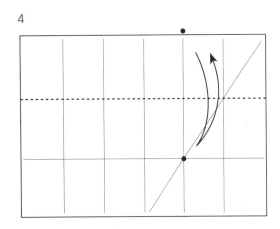

5

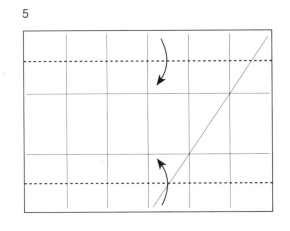

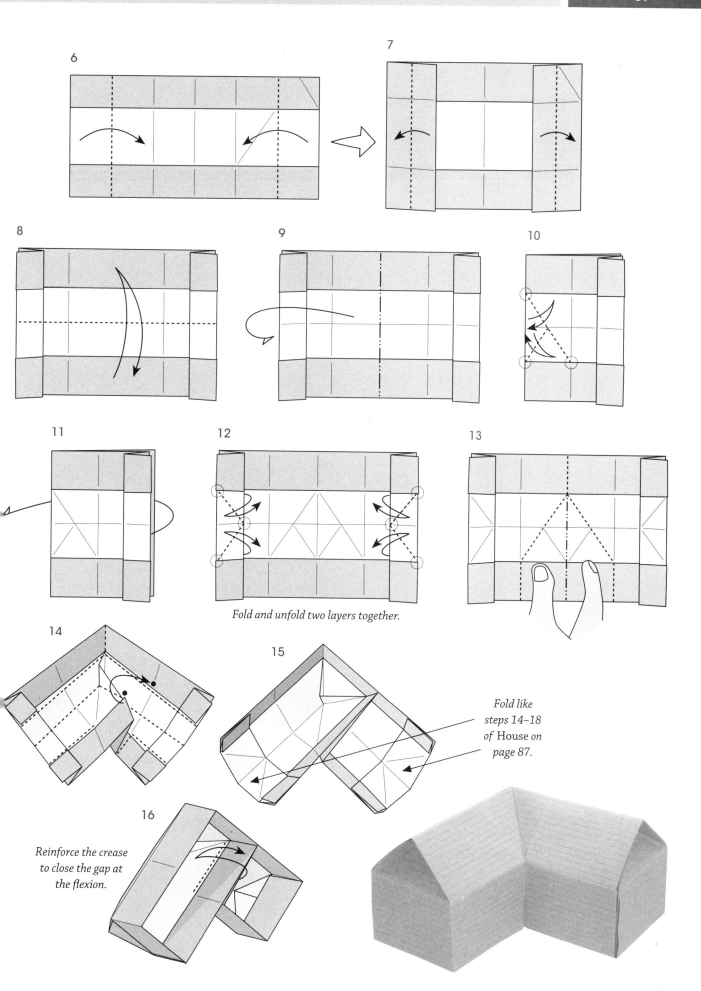

6

7

8

9

10

11

12

Fold and unfold two layers together.

13

14

15

Fold like steps 14–18 of House on page 87.

16

Reinforce the crease to close the gap at the flexion.

18. RE-ROOFING

I designed various roofs because I wanted to change the color of the *House*'s roof.

A5	A5
Wall	*Gable Roof*
A5	A5
Boat-shaped Roof	*Square Roof 1*
A4	A4 A7
Square Roof 2	*Dutch Gable*

Wall

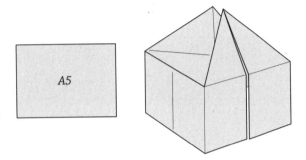

A5

Make a base of Silver Tower *on page 61.*

Gable Roof

1

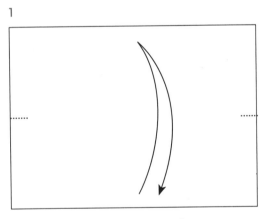

Pinch at the edges only.

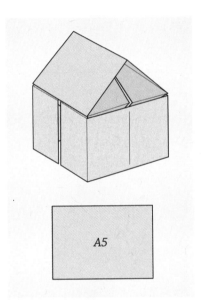

A5

2

3

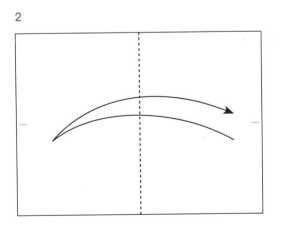

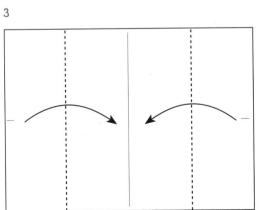

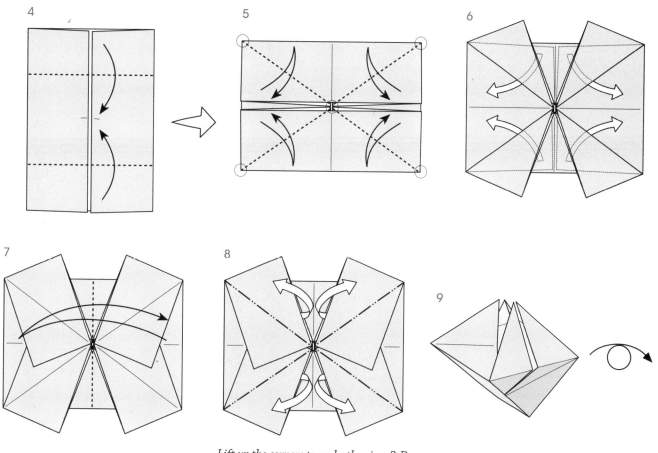

Lift up the corners to make the piece 3-D

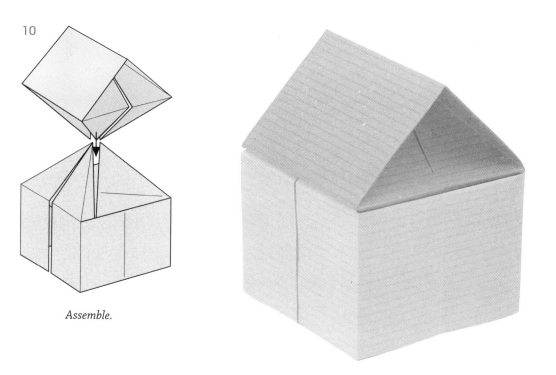

Assemble.

Boat-shaped Roof

This roof is typical of the Toraja area in Indonesia, which is famous for its coffee. The real roof is more rounded.

It also resembles house-shaped Haniwa, ancient Japanese clay figures that were buried in tumuli.

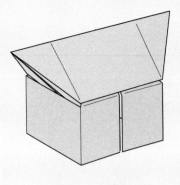

1

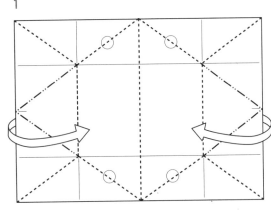

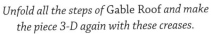

Unfold all the steps of Gable Roof *and make the piece 3-D again with these creases.*

2

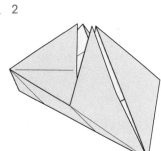

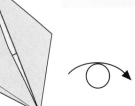

3

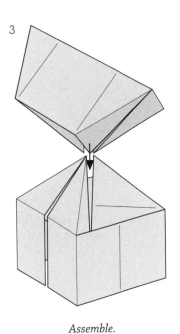

Assemble.

Square Roof 1

It is one type of the pavilion roof. The *Non-sunken Honeycomb Octahedron* (page 46) has the same shape, though it will not make a steady house.

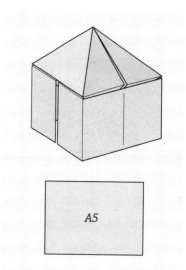

A5

1

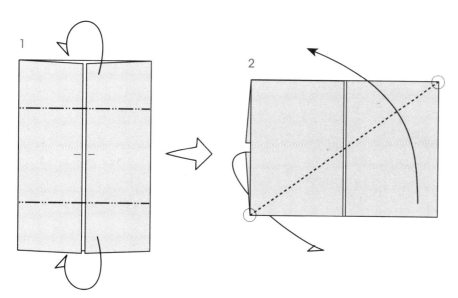

Start from step 4 of
Gable Roof *on page 91.*

2

3

4

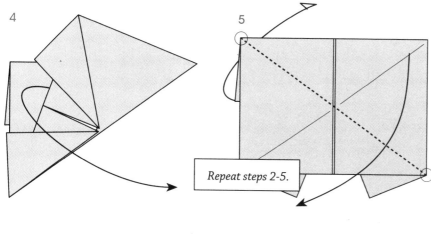

5

Repeat steps 2-5.

6

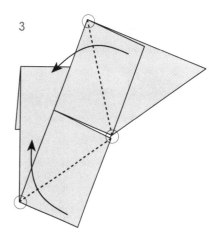

7

8

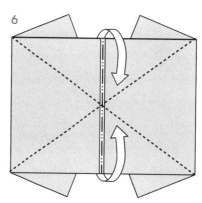

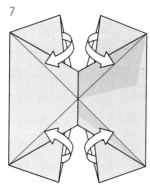

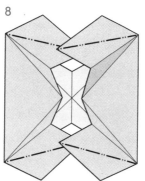

9

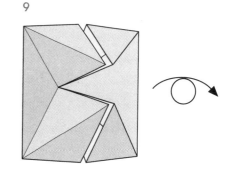

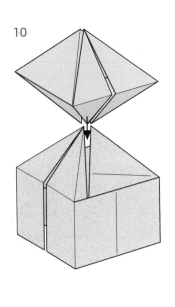

10

I was somewhat dissatisfied with the roof as it looked leaky because of the slits. Also, I wanted to make eaves, so I designed another square roof.

Square Roof 2

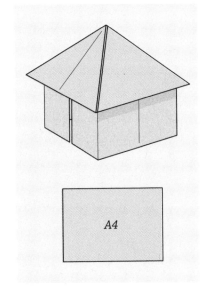

A4

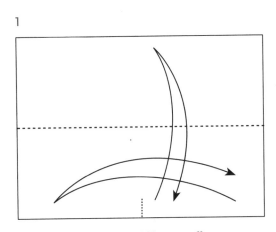

1

Fold and unfold horizontally and pinch at the bottom.

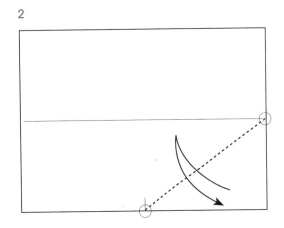

2

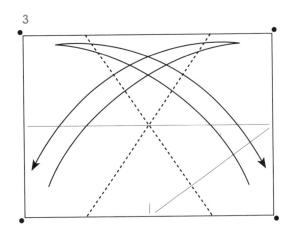

3

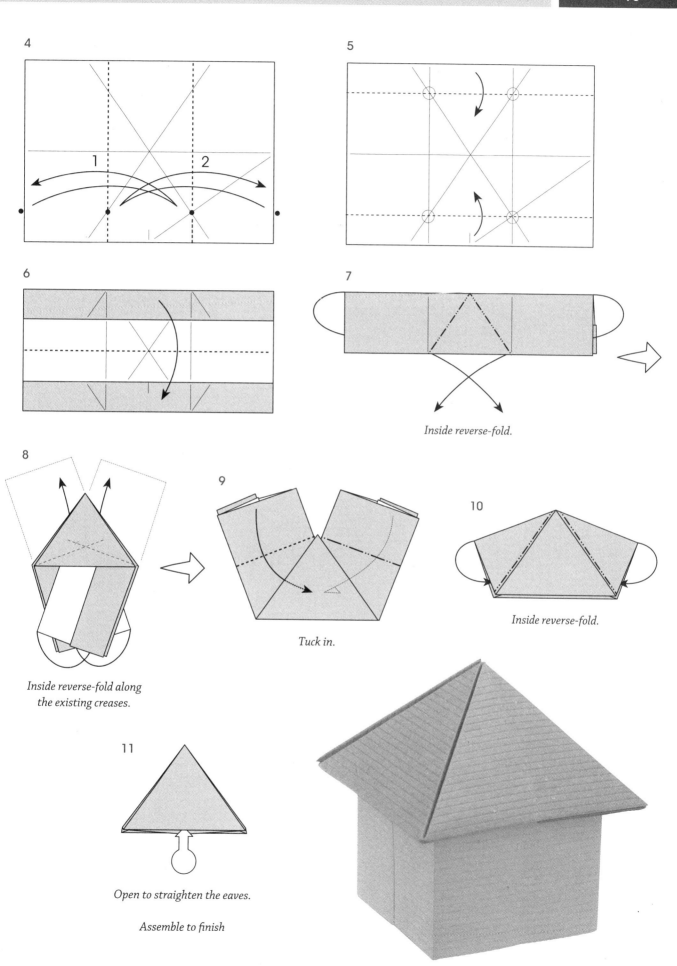

4

5

6

7

Inside reverse-fold.

8

Inside reverse-fold along
the existing creases.

9

Tuck in.

10

Inside reverse-fold.

11

Open to straighten the eaves.

Assemble to finish

Dutch Gable

1

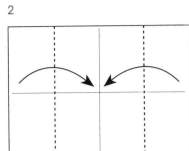

2

3

4

5

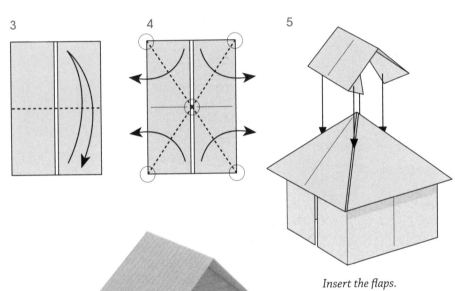

Insert the flaps.

A4, make a
Square Roof 2.

+

A7

*Use an A7 (one
eighth of A4) sheet.*

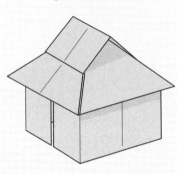

ROOF TYPES

Besides the roofs presented here, typical roof types includes the flat roof, the sawtooth roof often used for factories, the butterfly roof that is the valley-folded (reversed) gable roof, the pent roof that consists of a single slope, the dome roof, and the most basic hip roof. The square roof can be seen as a kind of hip roof, that is, the hip roof for a square building. I am going to present the hip roof on the next page.

All the roofs diagramed here have slopes at 45 degrees since they are designed based on √2 and the cube. Real roofs usually have more gentle slopes.

DIFFERENT ASSEMBLING

You can assemble these roof modules, as well as the modules of *Honeycomb Octahedron* on page 40, *Honeycomb Octahedron in Coordinate System* on page 48, and *Silver Tower* on page 61, in different ways to make various polyhedra, some of which can tessellate the three-dimensional space. Enjoy building the polyhedra as a puzzle to feel space-filling structures.

POLYHEDRA MADE OF ROOF MODULES

| Square roof 1 + Square roof 1 → an octahedron | Square roof 1 + Boat-shaped roof → a quarter of a rhombic dodecahedron | Boat-shaped roof + Boat-shaped roof → a tetrahedron | Gable roof + Gable roof → "Bi-roofed Polyhedron" |

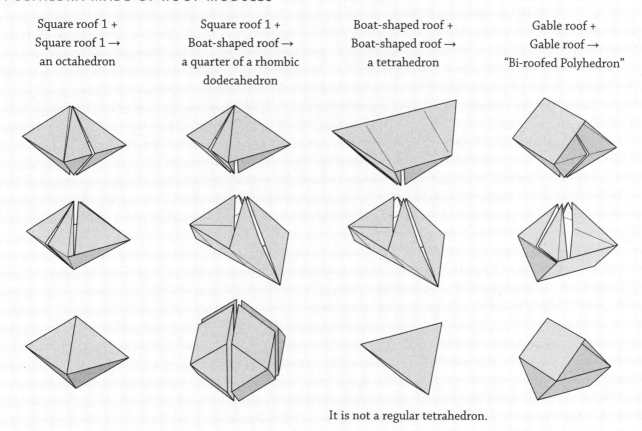

It is not a regular tetrahedron.

19. HIP ROOF

You can add a chimney that is made of a separate sheet.

A4, two sheets

Main Part

1

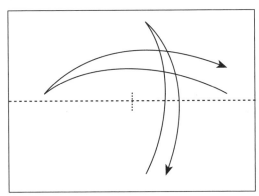

Fold and unfold horizontally and pinch at the center. (Use a sheet with a different color from the roof.)

2

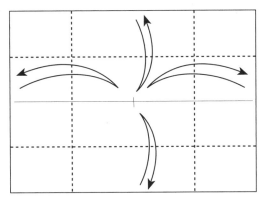

3

4

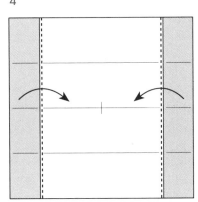

5

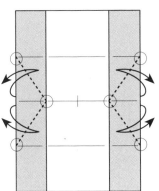

Fold and unfold all layers together.

6

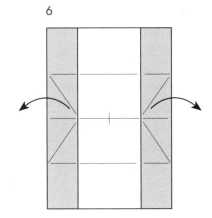

Unfold back to step 4.

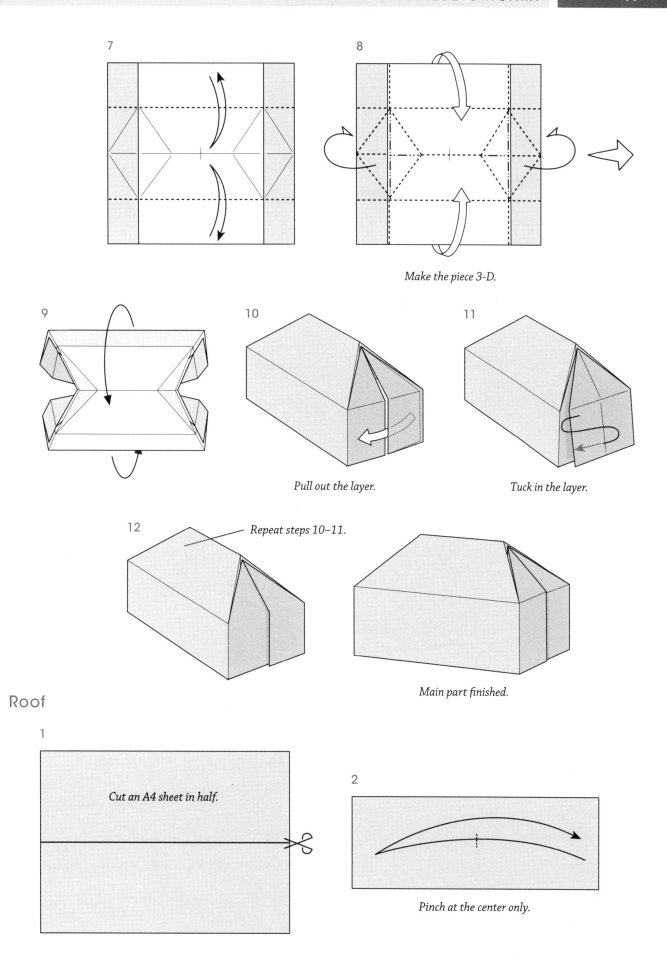

7

8

Make the piece 3-D.

9

10

Pull out the layer.

11

Tuck in the layer.

12 Repeat steps 10–11.

Main part finished.

Roof

1

Cut an A4 sheet in half.

2

Pinch at the center only.

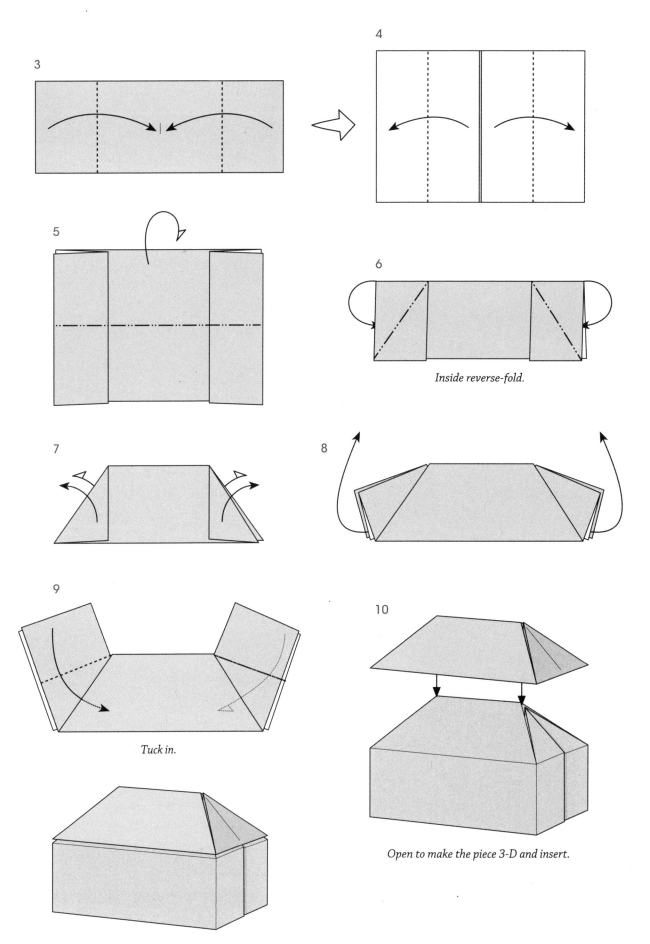

3

4

5

6

Inside reverse-fold.

7

8

9

Tuck in.

10

Open to make the piece 3-D and insert.

Chimney

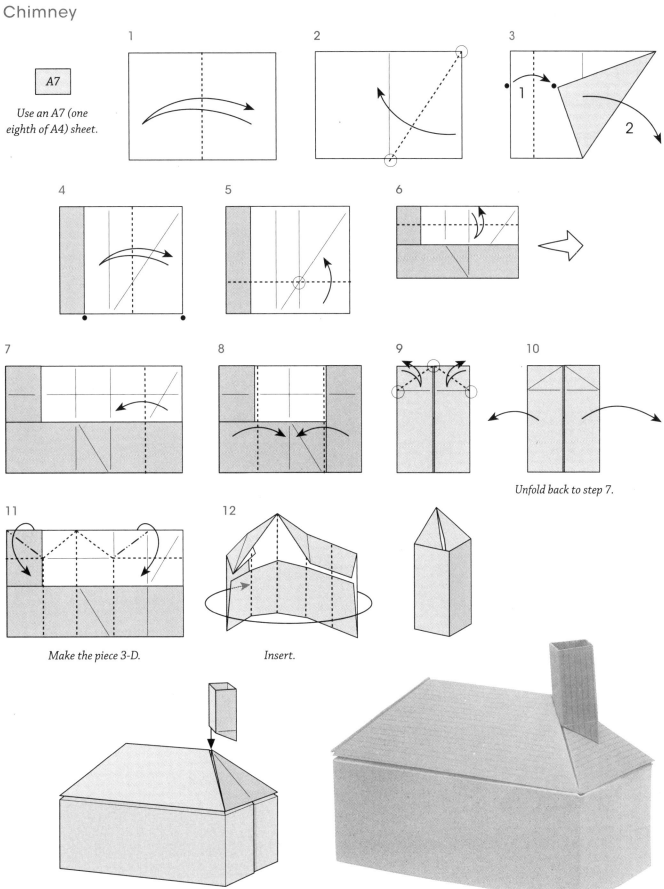

A7

Use an A7 (one eighth of A4) sheet.

Unfold back to step 7.

Make the piece 3-D.

Insert.

Insert.

20. PENTA-HEPTA-HEXAHEDRON

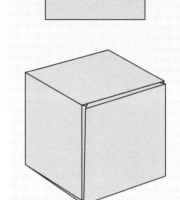

A4

This model is not based on the ratio √2 but 7/5, an approximation of √2.

1

210mm

3mm
(actual size)

297mm

*Fold by 3 mm to make the
aspect ratio 5:7 (the folded part
is not shown in the diagrams).*

2

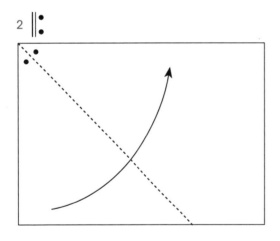

3

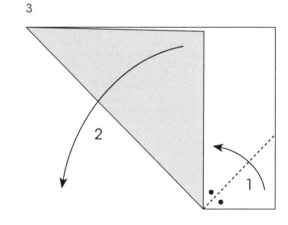

4

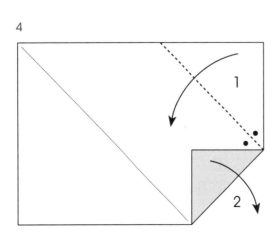

5

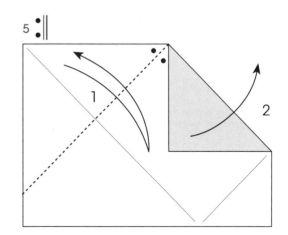

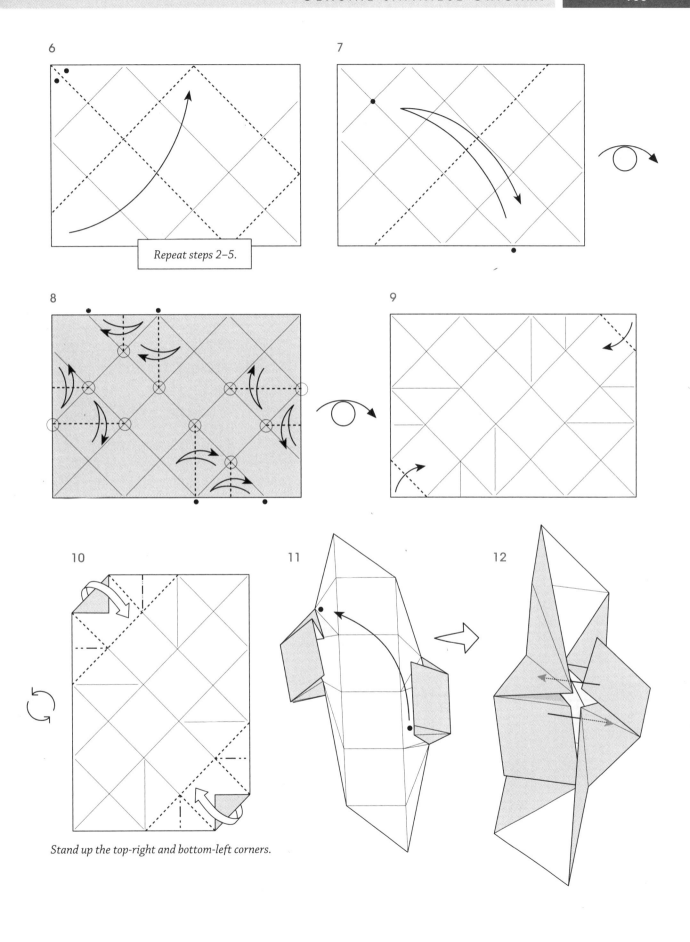

6

Repeat steps 2–5.

7

8

9

10

Stand up the top-right and bottom-left corners.

11

12

13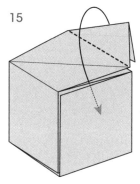

14

15

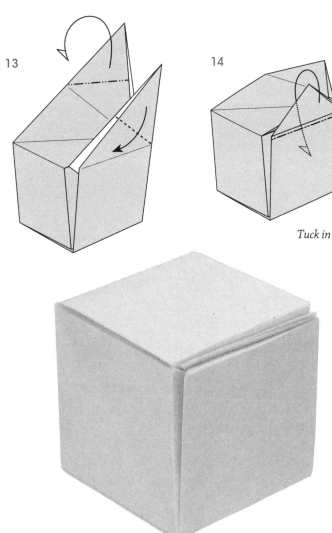

Tuck in the flap to finish.

ORIGAMI MODELS RELATED TO THE CUBE

Unlike the previous octahedra, cubes, rhombic dodecahedra, or roof-shaped models, *Penta-hepta-hexahedron* is not based on √2 itself. The next four models are also different from previous ones, even though they pertain to the cube. They do not have diagonal creases of silver rectangles, those creases you have folded many times in the previous models. Rather, they have creases that run in 22.5 degrees or the "matching angle" of the silver rectangle.

DEVELOPMENT OF THE CUBE

We have 11 types of the development of the cube, each of which consists of six squares. The model on page 102, *Penta-hepta-hexahedron*, is based on the first one in the top row.

Note that the four types in the top row are rotationally symmetric.

Satoshi Degawa designed another cube that is published in Kunihiko Kasahara's *Chohokei-de Oru (Fold with Rectangles)* using the first type in the second row. His model is based on the equation $3/4 + \alpha = \sqrt{2}$ and has a straightforward sequence. (Actually, it happens to be exactly the same as my unpublished model *Postcard Cube*.)

The length of a side of *Penta-hepta-hexahedron* is shorter than that of his cube, but it is interestingly very close to that of my cubes based on √2, such as *Loop Hole Cube* on page 71, *One-third Cube* on page 79, and *Box with Cat Ears* on the next page. Let the silver rectangle have the shorter side of length 1, and the length of a side of *Penta-hepta-hexahedron* is about 0.2828 whereas that of other cubes is about 0.2928. The difference is around 2 mm in A4 sheets.

Squares that will be the faces of Penta-hepta-hexahedron.

Development of the cube.

21. BOX WITH CAT EARS

I came up with this title because the model has projections that look like cat ears. The lower part is a cube.

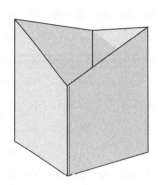

1

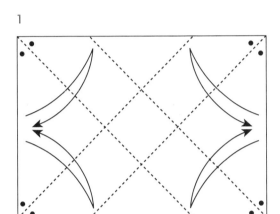

2

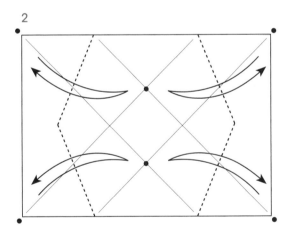

3

Rabbit-ear fold.

4

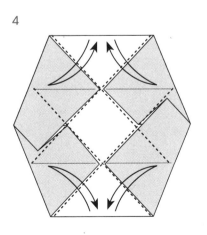

5

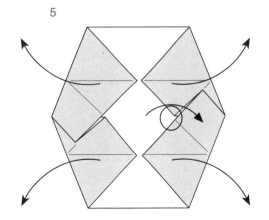

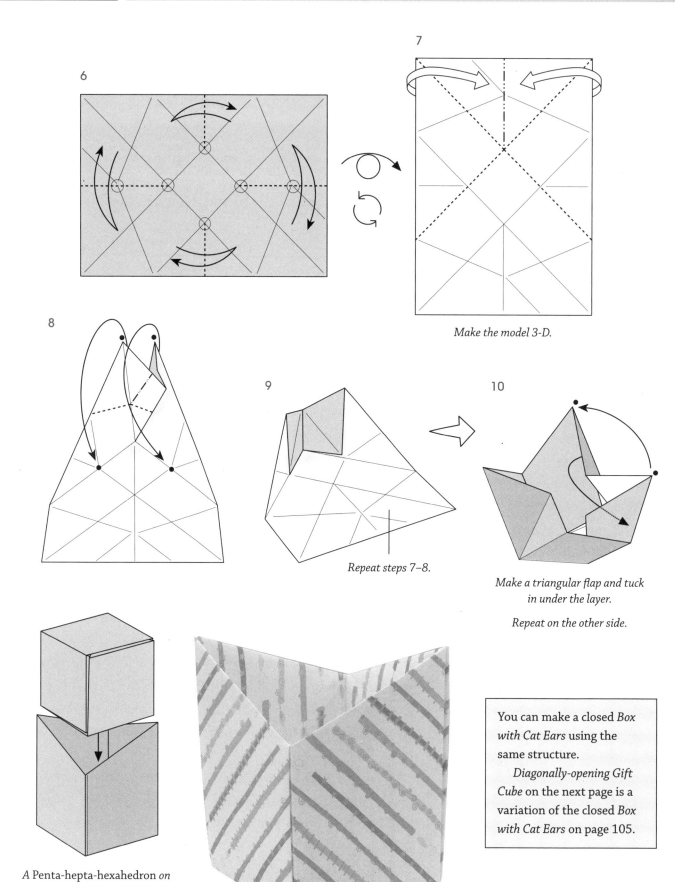

6

7

Make the model 3-D.

8

9

Repeat steps 7–8.

10

Make a triangular flap and tuck in under the layer.

Repeat on the other side.

A Penta-hepta-hexahedron *on the previous page will fit nicely.*

You can make a closed *Box with Cat Ears* using the same structure.

Diagonally-opening Gift Cube on the next page is a variation of the closed *Box with Cat Ears* on page 105.

22. DIAGONALLY-OPENING GIFT CUBE

This practical model is suitable for a gift box as it is relatively easy to open and close. Using heavy sheets is recommended.

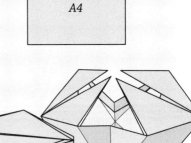

1

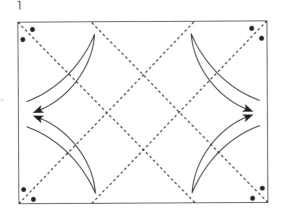

2

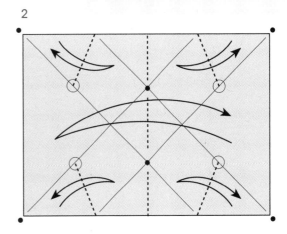

3

4

5

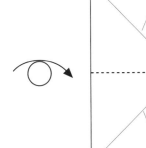

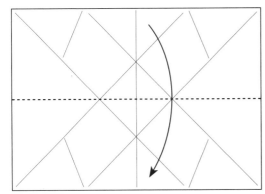

Inside reverse-fold.
(The layers will be like a fan.)

6

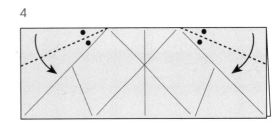

7

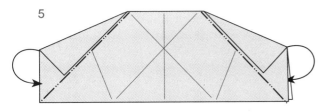

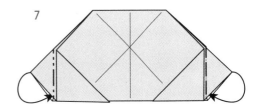

Inside reverse-fold.

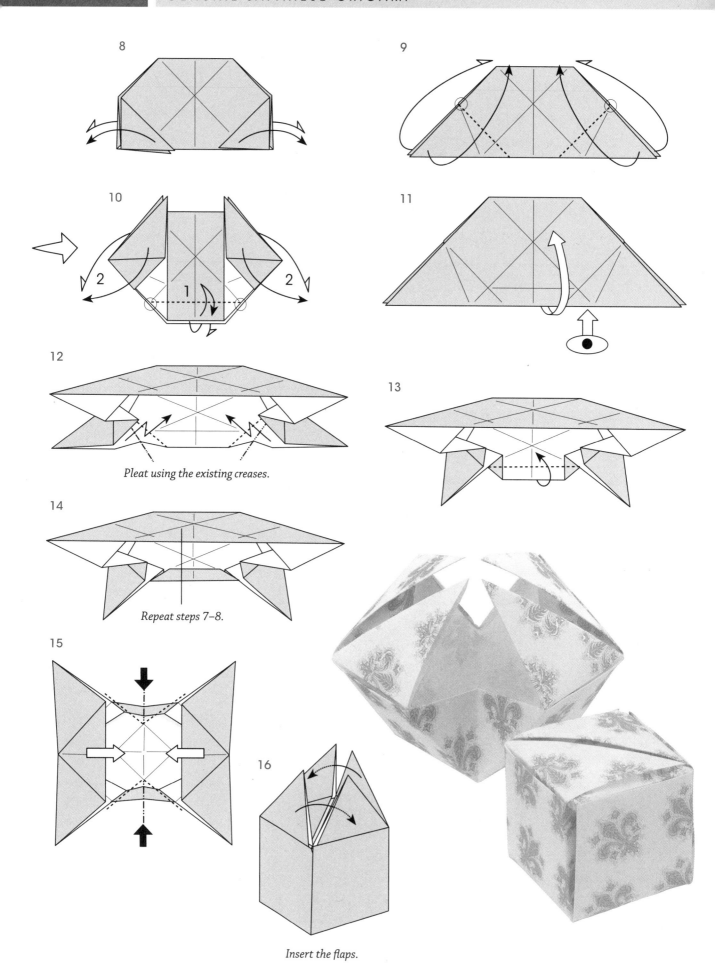

8

9

10

11

12

Pleat using the existing creases.

13

14

Repeat steps 7–8.

15

16

Insert the flaps.

23. BOX WITH HANDLES

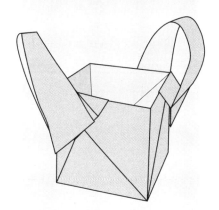

A4

Step 12 of the model would be *Tsuno-darai* or four-handled basin from the Heian period, which was believed to turn into a monster.

1

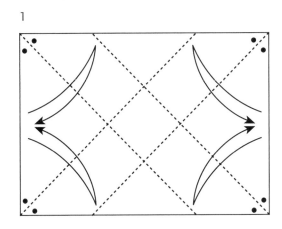

2

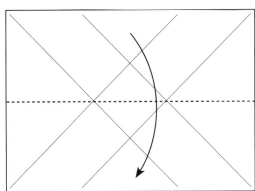

3

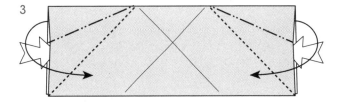

4

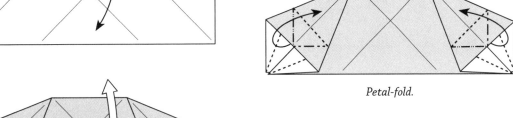

Petal-fold.

5

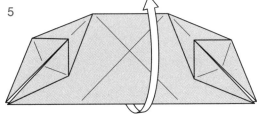

Unfold all the steps.

6

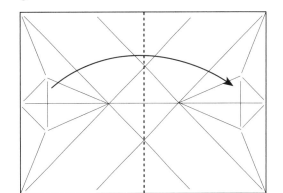

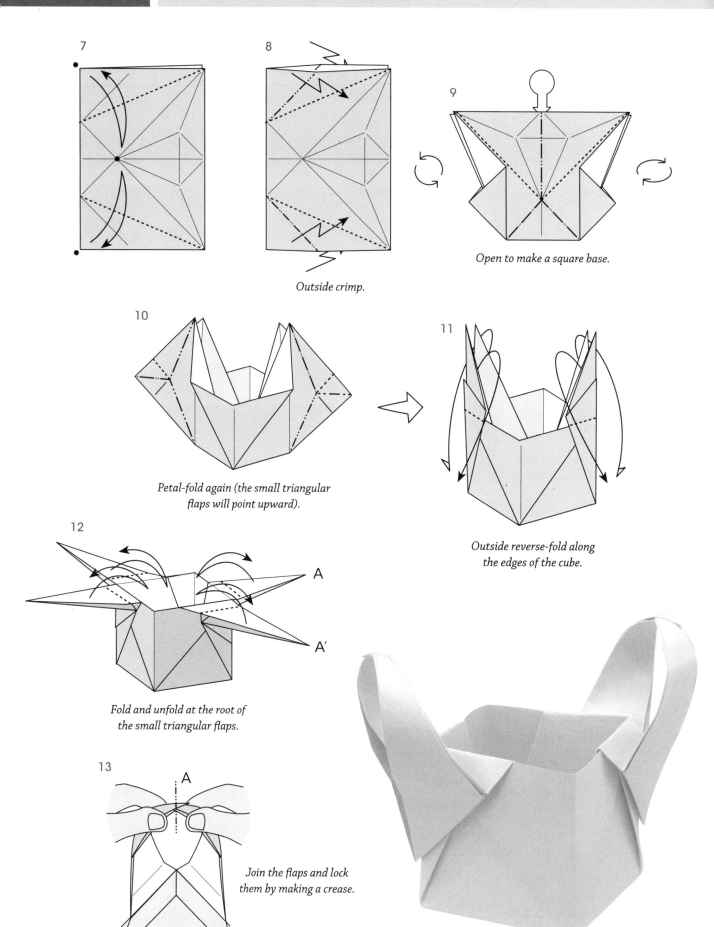

7

8

Outside crimp.

9

Open to make a square base.

10

Petal-fold again (the small triangular
flaps will point upward).

11

Outside reverse-fold along
the edges of the cube.

12

A

A′

Fold and unfold at the root of
the small triangular flaps.

13

A

Join the flaps and lock
them by making a crease.

24. CUBE MASU BOX

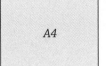

A4

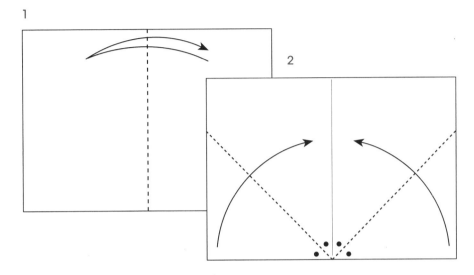

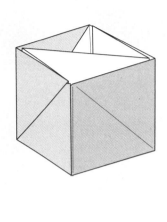

1

2

3

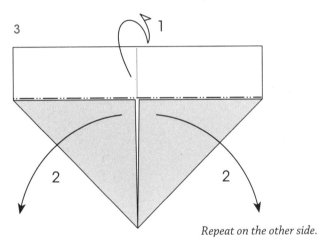

Repeat on the other side.

4

5

Repeat on the other side.

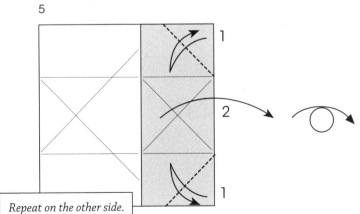

6

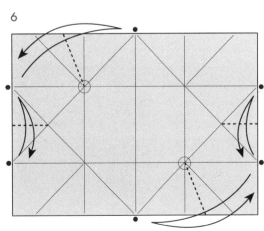

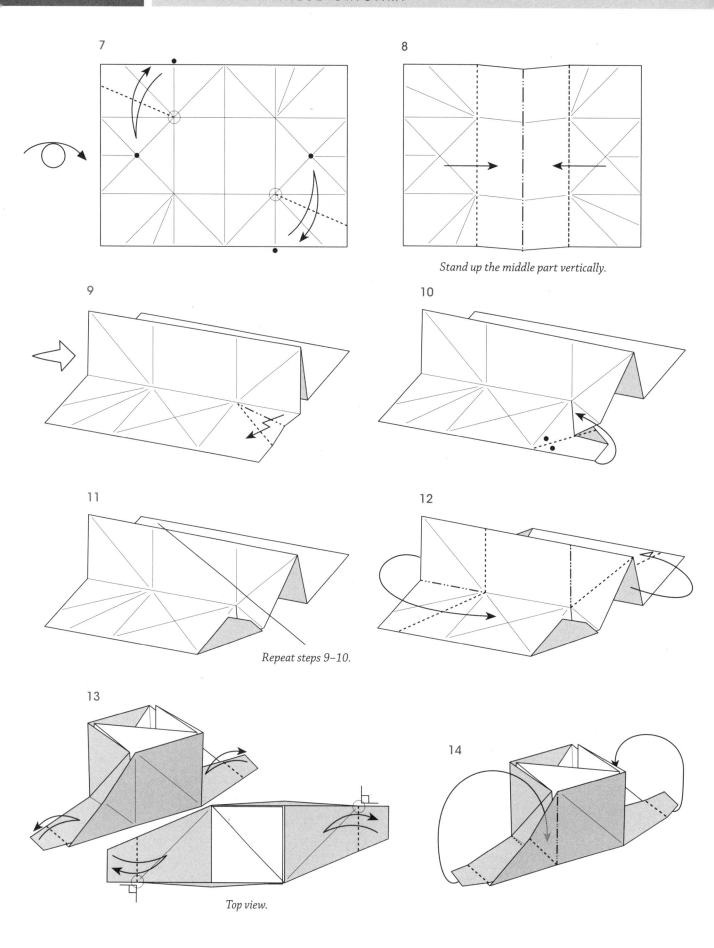

7

8

Stand up the middle part vertically.

9

10

11

Repeat steps 9–10.

12

13

Top view.

14

15

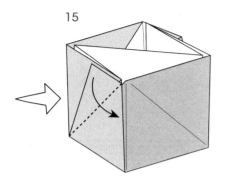

16

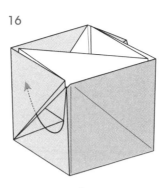

Tuck in.

Repeat behind.

17

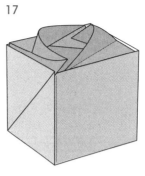

You can put in a Half Z Cube *on page 73 or a* Cube Rose *on the next page folded with half-sized sheets.*

25. CUBE ROSE

Use sheets with the same color on both sides, though the colors are different in the diagrams.

A5, two sheets

LEAVES AND CALYCES

1

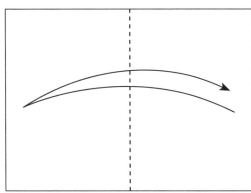

2

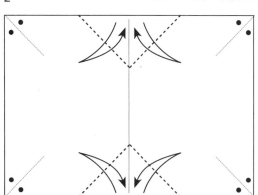

Make creases at the middle part only.

3

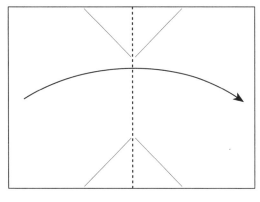

4

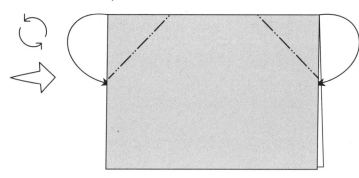

Inside reverse-fold.

5

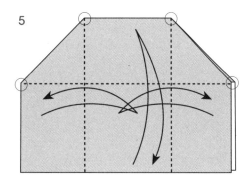

Repeat behind.

6

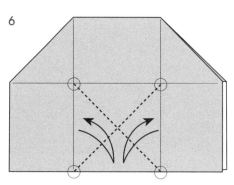

Repeat behind.

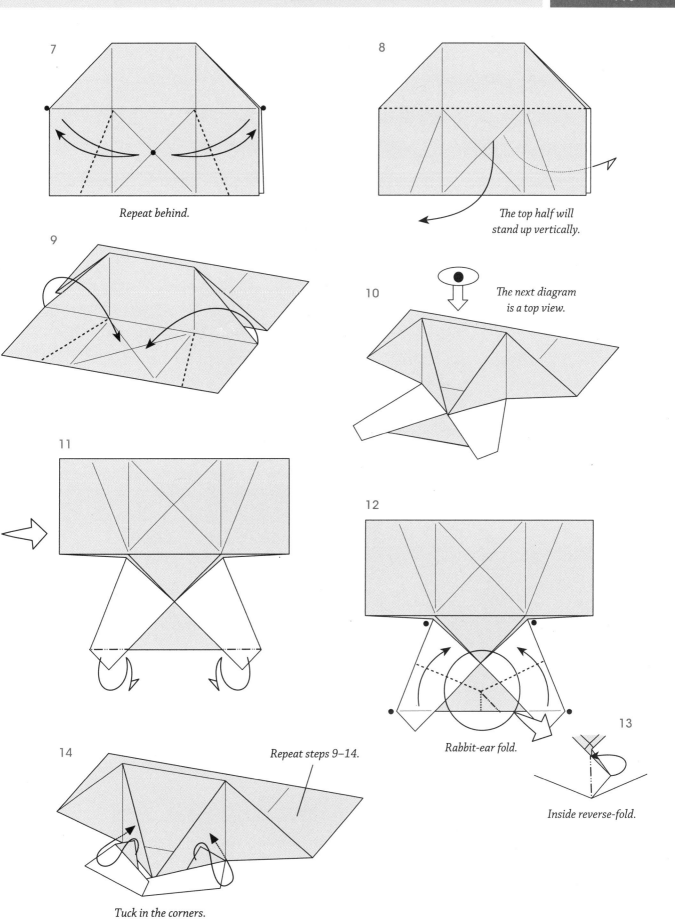

7

Repeat behind.

8

The top half will stand up vertically.

9

10

The next diagram is a top view.

11

12

Rabbit-ear fold.

13

Inside reverse-fold.

14

Repeat steps 9–14.

Tuck in the corners.

FLOWER

1

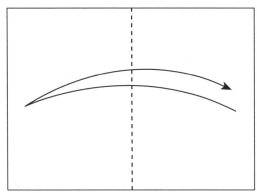

2

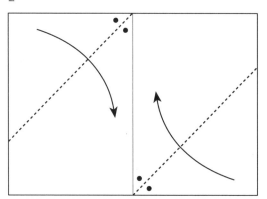

3

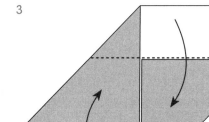

4

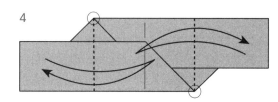

5

6

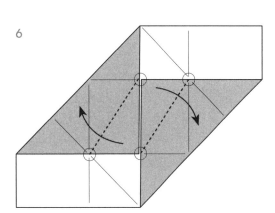

7

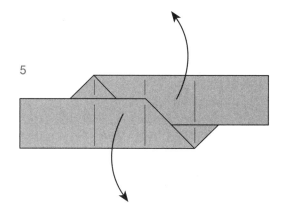

8

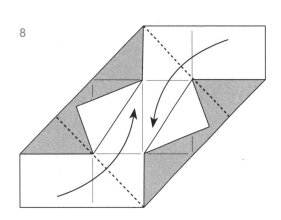

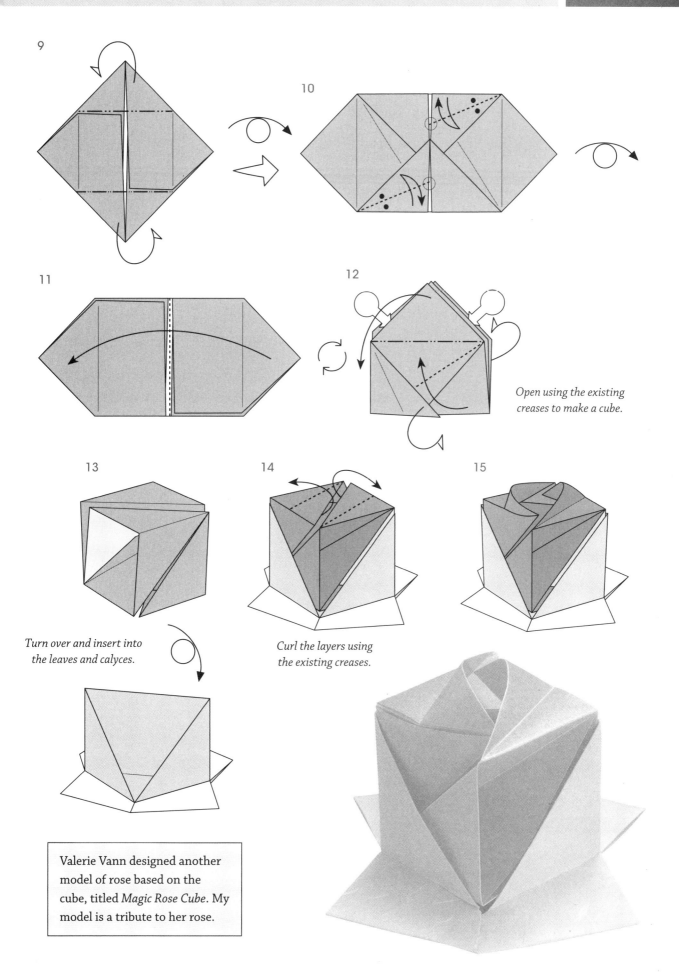

9

10

11

12

Open using the existing
creases to make a cube.

13

Turn over and insert into
the leaves and calyces.

14

Curl the layers using
the existing creases.

15

Valerie Vann designed another
model of rose based on the
cube, titled *Magic Rose Cube*. My
model is a tribute to her rose.

26. ISO-AREA HALF-COOKED CUBE

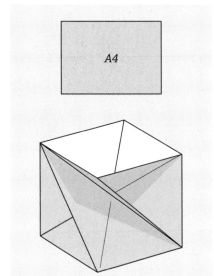

A4

The model is an example of "iso-area" folding, a notion introduced by Toshikazu Kawasaki. It is titled "Half-cooked" because it looks an unfinished cube for me. It makes different impressions when viewed from different angles.

1

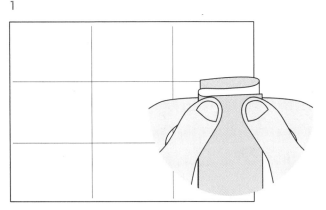

Trisect the sides both horizontally and vertically.

Although I have explained how to trisect a side in *Triple Spiral Cube* on page 69, I recommend folding by "guessing" as shown in the figure for the model since we do not want extra creases.

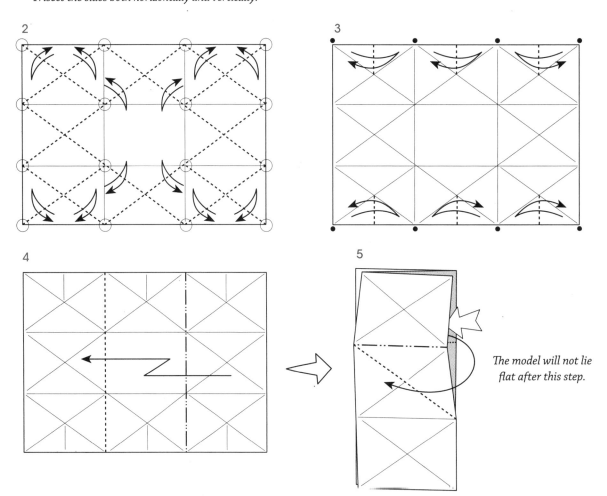

2

3

4

5

The model will not lie flat after this step.

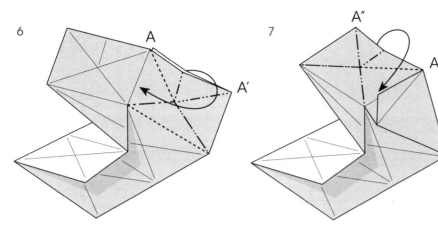

6

7

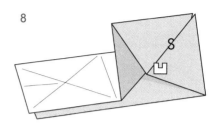

8

Fold two layers together to make a pyramid.

Make a pyramid.

The flaps made in steps 6 and 7 are tucked in slit S.

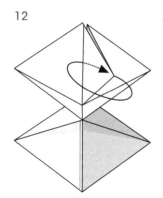

9

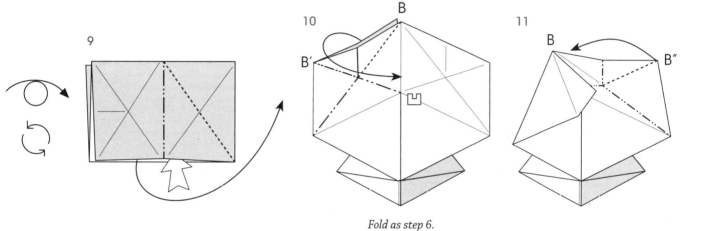

10

11

Fold as step 6.

12

Tuck in the flap.

CUBE SECTIONS

An iso-area origami model is a model such that alternating the mountain and valley folds does not change its form. The cube is a suitable subject for iso-area folding because it is one of most symmetrical solids. In fact, the first iso-area model designed by Toshikazu Kawasaki is also a cube. You may be able to design different iso-area cubes by looking at sections of the cube.

I designed the model on the previous page using the fact that one of cube sections is a silver rectangle. You can utilize the sections shown below to design your own model. Here I would like to present the most "beautiful" iso-area cube of my design, although it is not made of a silver rectangle sheet but a sheet in irregular shape. It is based on the regular hexagonal section of the cube (see the right figure below).

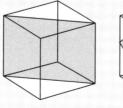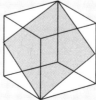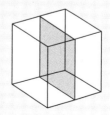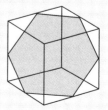

Symmetrical sections of the cube.

Iso-area Hexa-cube (Reference)

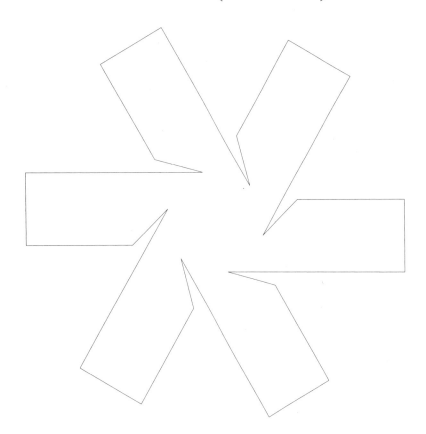

1

Enlarge the template and cut along the lines. A transparent sheet will work very well.

2

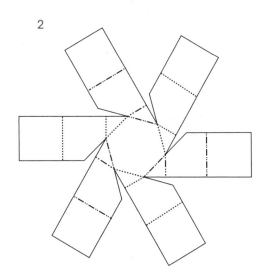

Make creases as shown above and put three flaps together on each side.

Make with a transparent sheet and use as a gift box for a pin badge and the like.

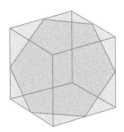

All the six faces of the cube have two layers.

27. ONE-THIRD CUBE (SQUARE VERSION) AND THE DIE IS SPLIT

Following a model made of an irregular-shaped sheet, I would like to present two models made of square sheets. I designed both of them using diagonal creases of silver rectangles, as many models in this chapter. In fact, I have designed a lot of such models and selected the best two.

One of them has exactly the same shape as *One-third Cube* on page 79.

The other is a cube split in half, hence the title *The Die Is Split*. I show only the crease pattern as a challenging puzzle.

ONE-THIRD CUBE (SQUARE VERSION)

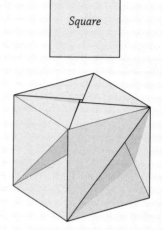

Square

THE DIE IS SPLIT

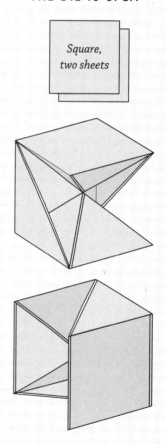

Square, two sheets

1

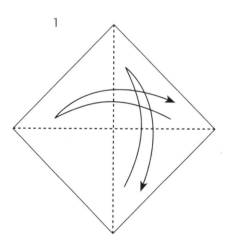

2

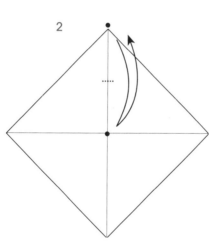

3

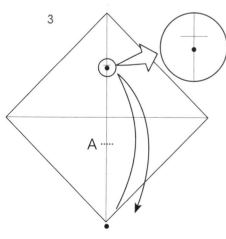

2.3 mm (0.09 in) when using 15 cm (6 in) sheet. (The diagram in the circle is in the actual size.)

A

Fold to the point about 2.3 mm below the crease when using a 15 cm square sheet.

4

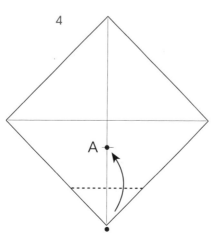

A

Instead of approximating as shown above, you can find the accurate reference point in this way.

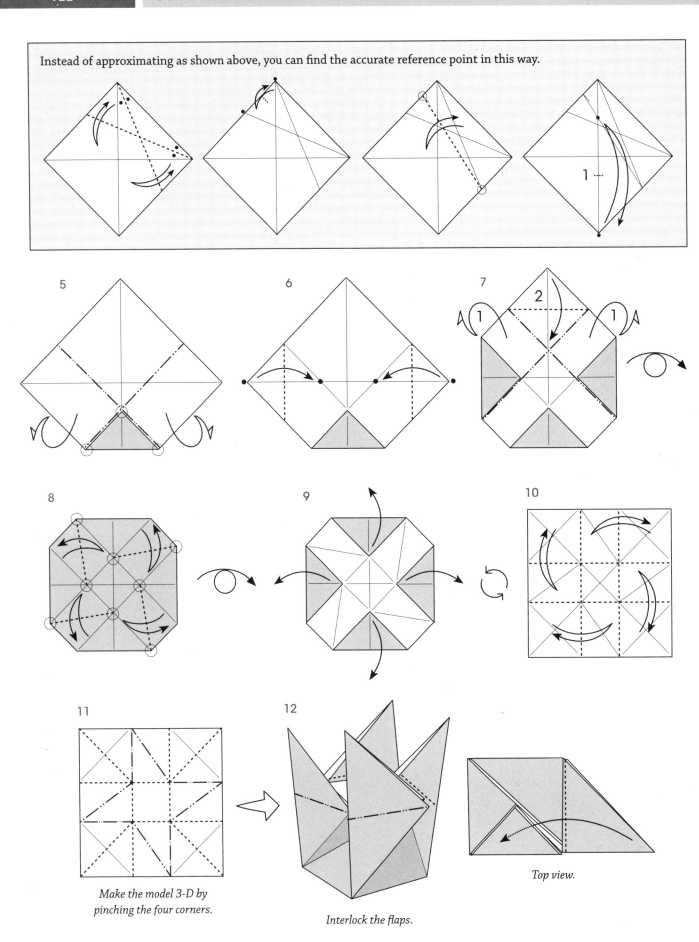

5

6

7

8

9

10

11

Make the model 3-D by pinching the four corners.

12

Interlock the flaps.

Top view.

The Die is Split

Find the reference point in almost the same way as One-third Cube on page 79.

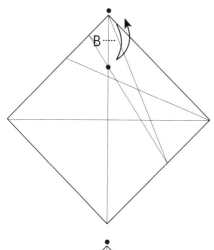

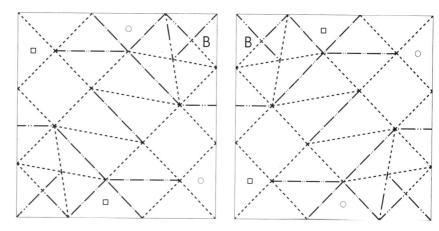

Fold to the point about 2.3 mm (0.09 in) below one quarter of the diagonal when using a 15 cm (6 in) square sheet, as step 3 on page 121.

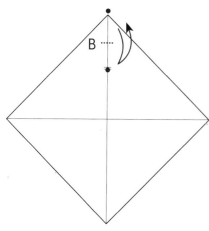

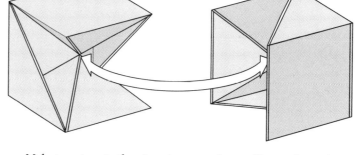

Make two pieces in the mirror images and assemble to make a cube.

Place one of the two white circles onto the other, and do the same with the white squares. The volume of one piece will be one half of the cube.

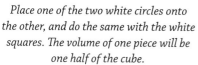

³√2 (ABE'S CONSTRUCTION)

It is rather perplexing to find the reference point for the models on the previous page. Still, we are folding a ratio that is a combination of the square root and integers.

Hisashi Abe found that we can construct a cube root by folding paper. To conclude the chapter, I would like to briefly introduce his construction of the cube root of 2.

The construction of the cube root of 2 is equivalent to the construction of the length of a side of a cube that has the volume twice as large as a given cube. The problem, called Delian problem, is as old as ancient Greece.

It was proved in the nineteenth century that the length is not constructible with ruler and compass. With origami, however, we can construct it using a fold that place a point on a line and another point on another line.

Refer to his book *Sugoizo Origami* for detailed explanation of the construction.

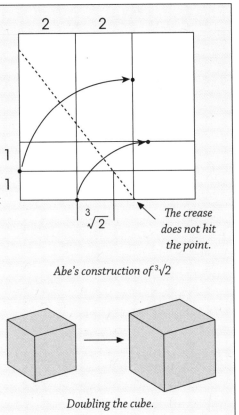

Abe's construction of ³√2

Doubling the cube.

SEEING IN YOUR HEAD

So, that was chapter 3 on the silver rectangle and the cube. I hope you have enjoyed it.

The models are somewhat different from other origami models such as flowers and animals, but I believe they are fascinating exercises of your brain.

Denis Diderot (1713–1784), an exponent of French Enlightenment, wrote suggestive sentences about the solid explained in the chapter, "The pyramid that is a division of the cube," in his book *Letter on the Blind*, which treats epistemology through dialogues with a blind lady.

> She had insisted that geometry was really appropriate for blinds. That is because learning it requires only strong attention and because mastering it requires no assistance. She used to add that geometricians spend almost all of their life with their eyes closed. … One day I said to her, "Miss, imagine a regular hexahedron. — Sure, I've done it. — Now imagine a point at the center of the regular hexahedron. — I've done it. — Draw lines from the point to all the apices, and you divide the regular hexahedron. — Now I have identical six pyramids each of which has identical sides, a base that is a face of the cube, and the height half of the cube, added she. — That's right. But where do you see them? — In my head. And I think you do, too."

The cube appears to be simple, but it has inexhaustible attraction not only as a solid but also as a subject of origami. In fact, Kunihiko Kasahara has published the book *Origami Shinhakken 2: Cube-no Sekai (Origami Discovery 2: World of the Cube)* that is dedicated exclusively to the cube. The chapter is my own "world of the cube" based on the silver rectangle.

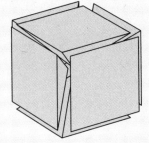

AFTERWORD

I decided to write this book as a sequel to my previous book *Genuine Origami*, after receiving more favorable responses than I had expected.

I had, however, a different motive for writing this book. For me, this book is what I have wanted to write, while the previous one was what I must write, though I did not have specific images for it. I have had a vague plan for over 20 years to write an origami book without including any models that are made from the square, and now I feel I have done it.

In the origami world, many regard making a model with a square sheet without cuts as the highroad of origami. In addition, many seem to regard me as one of the advocators of that "school." Although I am sure the square is a special form in origami, I do not persist in folding square sheets. What I want to feel with my hands, eyes, and brain is the world of harmony consisting of surfaces and lines, and one can see the world more clearly by taking a step back from the square.

With such ideas in my mind, I thought I didn't have enough time to write another book with my busy schedule. Now I find that anyone seems to be able to have some time somehow. I was just lazy. Such a lazy man could not complete a whole book without direct and indirect encouragement from pioneers and peers, utmost proofreading done by my wife Sumiko, and feedback from the readers of the previous book. Feeling somewhat awkward, I must say a formal "thank you" to all of them.

I also thank the photographer Kazuhisa Okuyama, the designer Fukura Yanagihara, and the editor Yasushi Takado for their patient cooperation. I think I have been a troublesome author cramming more diagrams than the previous book, wandering through so many topics that the proofreading was painful, increasing the number of models by about $\sqrt{2}$ times, and even working on the bookbinding.

Last but not least, I thank all of you readers for putting your hands on the book. Hoping that each of you will spend joyful times with it, I would like to give the book to the world with butterflies in my stomach.

Jun Maekawa, feeling the autumn breeze of 2009

INDEX

REFERENCES

Maekawa, Jun; Kasahara, Kunihiko ed. *Viva! Origami*, Sanrio, 1983.

Maekawa, Jun. *Honkaku Origami*, Japan Publications, 2007 (English edition: Maekawa Jun; Hatori, Koshiro and Noguchi, Marcio tr. *Genuine Origami*, Japan Publications Trading, 2008).

Kasahara, Kunihiko. *Chohokei-de Oru*, Japan Publications, 2007.

Kasahara, Kunihiko. *Copy-yoshi-de Oru*, Japan Publications, 2007.

Kasahara, Kunihiko. *Super Chohokei Origami*, Japan Publications, 2009.

Nakamura, Eiji. *Soratobu Origami Kessaku 30-sen*, Japan Publications, 1973.

Nakamura, Eiji. *Etoki Shinpo Origami*, Ikeda Publishing, 1975.

Ohashi, Koya. *Chohokei-no Origami*, Kairyudo Publishing, 1978.

Abe, Hisashi. *Sugoizo Origami*, Nippon Hyoronsha, 2003.

Nakamura, Shigeru. *Fibonacci-su-no Sho-uchu* (revised edition), Nippon Hyoronsha, 2002.

Saito, Ken. *Euclid "Genron"-toha nanika* Iwanami Shoten, 2008.

Fukagawa, Hidetoshi. *Reidai-de Shiru Nihon-no Sugaku-to Sangaku*, Morikita Publishing, 1998.

Miyazaki, Koji. *Kenchiku-no Katachi Hyakka*, Shokokusha, 2000.

Yanagi, Ryo. *Zoku Ogon Bunkatsu*, Bijutsu Shuppan-sha, 1977.

Sakurai, Susumu. *Setsugetsuka-no Sugaku*, Shodensha, 2006.

Adachi, Tsuneo. *√2-no Fushigi*, Kobunsha, 1994.

Flannery, David; Sato, Kaori and Sato, Hiroki tr. *√2-no Mori-to Andrew Shonen*, Springer, Japan, 2008 (Original edition: Flannery, David *The Square Root of 2*, Praxis Publishing, 2005).

Kobayashi, Kiyoomi. *Kami-no Sunpokikaku-to Sono Seitei-no Keii-nitsuite*, Paper Museum, 1985.

Tatsuno City Museum of History and Culture. *Oru Kokoro*, Tatsuno City Museum of History and Culture, 1999.

Takaki, Ryuji. *Katachi-no Jiten*, Maruzen, 2003.

PERIODICALS ON ORIGAMI

Origami Tanteidan, Japan Origami Academic Society (bimonthly).

Origami, Nippon Origami Association (monthly).

WEBSITES ON ORIGAMI

Origami Tanteidan, Japan Origami Academic Society, http://www.origami.gr.jp

Nippon Origami Association, Nippon Origami Association, http://www.origami-noa.com

PAPER USED FOR THE MODELS AT THE BEGINNING OF THE BOOK

Money Gift Wrapper: A4 OK Sand
Yin Yang Box: postcard-sized Hoshi-monogatari and taireishi
Trash Bin: A4 wrapping paper
Plate: A4 Tanto
Octagon Wrapper: B4 Leathac 66*, A4 OK Sand
Honeycomb Octahedron: A6 Rome Stone
One-sheet Honeycomb Octahedron: A4 Rome Stone
Non-sunken Honeycomb Octahedron: A7 Shin-kusakizome
Honeycomb Octahedron in Coordinate System: A5 Rome Stone
Honeycomb Octahedron in Intersecting Square Prisms: A5 Shin-kusakizome
Inverted Cube / Rhombic Dodecahedron / Cube Skeleton: A4 Shin-kusakizome
Two-sheet Sunken Rhombic Dodecahedron: A4 transparency
Silver Tower: A4 transparency and A4 Rome Stone
Silver Honeycomb: A4 Opal
Triple Spiral Cube: A4 Opal
Loop Hole Cube: A4 OK Feather Waltz
Half Z Cube: A5 Rome Stone

Plug-and-socket Puzzle Cube: A5 Curious Metal
One-third Cube: A4 OK Feather Waltz
Hexa-roofed Polyhedron: A5 Shin-rikyu
House: A4 flyer
L-shaped House: A4 Shin-rikyu
Re-roofing: A4 Shin-rikyu and others
Hip Roof: A4 Shin-rikyu and OK Sand
Penta-hepta-hexahedron: A4 Opal
Box with Cat Ears: A4 wrapping paper
Diagonally-opening Gift Cube: A4 wrapping paper
Box with Handles: A4 Curious Metal
Cube Masu Box: A4 Heisei
Cube Rose: A5 taireishi, Curious TL, and others
Iso-area Half-cooked Cube: A4 Boss Color*
Iso-area Hexa-cube: transparency
The Die Is Split: 15 cm (6 in) special origami paper

An asterisk (*) indicates the paper is difficult to fold because of the thickness or other reasons though it has nice texture

ABOUT THE AUTHOR

JUN MAEKAWA was born in Tokyo in 1958. He studied physics at Tokyo Metropolitan University. He is the executive officer and engineer at a science computation software company, a pioneer of technical origami design using crease patterns, a researcher on mathematics, science, history, and ethnology of origami, and a collector of items related to orizuru (origami crane).

He is the former president of Japan Origami Academic Society. He taught origami in Brazil appointed by the Japan Foundation in 1989, and co-administered the second International Meeting of Origami Science and Scientific Origami in 1994. He is a member of the Japan Origami Academic Society and The Astronomical Society of Japan.

He is the author of *Viva! Origami* (edited by Kunihiko Kasahara, Sanrio, 1983) and *Honkaku Origami* (Japan Publications, 2007) (English edition: *Genuine Origami*, translated by Koshiro Hatori and Marcio Noguchi, Japan Publications Trading, 2008) and the co-author of *Origami-no Suri-to Kagaku* (Toshikazu Kawasaki et al., Morikita Publishing, 2004) (original edition: Thomas Hull ed. *Origami*[3], A. K. Peters 2002) and other books.

Visit his blog at http://origami.asablo.jp